"Moy Hernandez, Jr. provides for the reader a most interesting, insightful, and illustrative narrative of the lives of some of the most important men and women of the Bible, drawing equally well from his own rich spiritual journey and strong Biblical teaching and principles. Though each were challenged in unique ways, these heroes of the faith proved to be overcomers, trusting in the Lord, and as a result, prove to be source of much inspiration to us in the present age. The logical conclusion for the reader will be, from my perspective, a desire to express and experience the faith, hope and Christlikeness that comes through a personal relationship with a triune and personal God who seeks fellowship with us. I am confident that the reader will be encouraged by the pages of this book for their own spiritual journey, wherever it may lead."

Edward Hill Commissioner
The Salvation Army

"This book is a guide for all those who feel like they have been stuck in the wilderness of life. It is a reminder of God's presence with us even when we feel that we are alone. It is the revelation that the wilderness is not just a detour in our journey but sometimes it is also the destination. Moy expertly unveils the story of Scripture as well as his own personal experiences to reveal a map in the wilderness and purpose in the wanderings. Moy speaks as one who has been there himself and is able to give firsthand insight for all of us along the way. Moy brings his true personality of sincerity, straightforwardness and humor to his writings as He intersects God's story and our stories to show us how we emerge from the place of being stuck to the place of being free."

Jordan Wong,
Senior Pastor
Almaden Neighborhood Church, San Jose, CA

THE
WILDERNESS
EXPERIENCE

A study on the road that leads to Faith,
Hope, and Christlikeness!

Moy Hernandez, Jr.

WESTBOW
P R E S S®
A DIVISION OF THOMAS NELSON
& ZONDERVAN

WestBow Press books may be ordered through booksellers or by contacting:

WestBow Press
A Division of Thomas Nelson & Zondervan
1663 Liberty Drive
Bloomington, IN 47403
www.westbowpress.com
844-714-3454

ISBN: 978-1-6642-3553-3 (sc)
ISBN: 978-1-6642-3552-6 (hc)
ISBN: 978-1-6642-3554-0 (e)

Library of Congress Control Number: 2021910643

Print information available on the last page.

WestBow Press rev. date: 07/06/2021

"This book is dedicated to the glory of God and the ongoing work of grace that He is performing in my life. You may come across some intentional grammatical issues or even misspelled words; they have been left in place on purpose to remind the reader that God is not quite done with us yet until we find ourselves in His eternal presence! Hang in there, God loves us despite our imperfections, He doesn't judge us for them, but is hard at work restoring us to His image, if you allow Him."

CONTENTS

PROLOGUE

I was born in paradise! Well, maybe around the corner from it. In Christopher Columbus' own words, I was born in the most beautiful place he had ever seen; yes, the beautiful Caribbean island of Cuba is my birthplace. And so it is from that place of beauty that I like to begin this book looking at not just my life, but the lives of others throughout Scripture, examining their own wilderness experience and how God brought them through that.

What do I mean when I say wilderness experience? It is a bit different for us all. Perhaps, it is a faith crisis or a time of loss, both physical and emotional, or just a time of silence in your walk with God. It can be a season of uncertainty, unanswered prayers, banishment, isolation, persecution, impossibility, suffering, shame, or maybe a time of incredible transformation, where the result is still uncleared. It may even be a time of unknowns, a time of spiritual brokenness, a time of living in the consequences of our past sin, where the only way out is through the path of repentance and contrition. It certainly could also be a time of significant loss, both the temporary separation from loved ones or the seemingly more permanent loss of life.

The medical world may even call it depression. Of course, there are also many different levels and experiences—feelings of sadness, fatigue, worthlessness, trouble in making decisions, insomnia, and even restlessness. However, I am not a medical doctor; therefore, my hope is not to diagnose some physical ailment that we may suffer from, but what I'd like to do is, look in God's Word in the hopes of understanding those times of dryness. As the Apostle James would put it, our seasons of uncertainty are a journey of trials and temptations. In the end, even if what we suffer from is a medical condition, God remains the great physician, and there is nothing He cannot bring us through or allow in our lives to get us to trust in Him more.

Here is a question for us to ponder as we begin: Do we personally cause these life-changing events in our lives, or are they solely God's design? Indeed, the Word of God reminds us in Romans 8:28 (CEB) that for "those who are called according to God's purpose, we know that God works all things together for good." A well-known and repeated Scripture verse, yet have we ever paused to ponder its meaning? This verse does not mean good in the sense of earthly comforts; instead, it is used in the context of Romans 8:29 (CEB), where we are reminded of our need to "conformed to the image of Christ." As a result, He will weave together all of our circumstances and happenstances to bring us to a closer fellowship with Christ. We will then bear good fruit (Galatians 5:22-23 CEB) for the kingdom of God and even carried on to verse 30 of Romans 28 (CEB), where we will be granted final justification and ultimate glorification in Heaven.

Because of these verses, I must be clear; I do not think God intends to get us out of our particular trials, at least not right away anyway. I believe He is more concerned with our eternal condition than our momentary discomforts. As a result, I pose to you that we are actively called into a spiritual wilderness; as a result of that call, we must endure those trials. More like survive them some of you may echo, they are purposeful and intentional life events, whether we caused them or God designs them. I believe this is why the Apostle James encourages us to "count it all joy when we go through trials of various kinds, for it is a simple test of our faith. Testing that will produce endurance and like an athlete that endurance will help us to mature in our faith, to be complete, to lack nothing" (James 1:3 CEB).

Which answers the question of why must we go through these

times of wilderness in the first place? Because God is verifying our faith to strengthen our commitment to Him. That He may produce in us a Christ-like character so that we may face life in complete dependence of God as our provider rather than on our feeble strength. But why must He test our faith at all? It is our nature to fail Him, to forget His love for us. Therefore, He seeks to humble us, not humiliate us, but truly make us more like His own son Jesus. Yes, of course, even in the depth of our anxiety, we cry out, LORD, it hurts. Father, I am in pain, dear Jesus, save me from this storm. Yet, all along, the lesson still must be learned. The character reinforcement must continue to take root! Where is our hope to be found in all of this? In the fact that God is gracious towards all of His children, as He reminds us in Scripture, that His Grace is always enough, always sufficient, always present. (2 Corinthians 12:9 CEB). The Apostle Paul testifies to this very thing in Romans 8:18 (CEB), where he declares his belief that "our present suffering is nothing compared to the coming glory that is going to be revealed to us."

I tend to believe these days that honesty and vulnerability are two ingredients that God often uses to strengthen our faith, and so I intend to be fully vulnerable with you. I do not seek your pity; but I hope to relate to your own wilderness experience. As I look at the length of my existence, I can see God working in many areas of my life, keeping me safe despite the many dumb things I've done along the way. Yet, what I have come to call my own wilderness experience; began to take shape around 2010 (yes, ten plus years in the making) when my relationship with my wife started to show signs of stress.

I was so preoccupied with what I thought was owed to me, what I thought I had earned through hard work in my ministry, that I sadly neglected many of my duties to what I have now recognized as my primary ministry, my family. Sure, there were good days, great family vacations, fantastic date nights, even ministerial success; but soon enough, the bad began to outnumber the good. Still, I ignored it by focusing on the wrong things, such as promotions, recognition, praise of others for my perceived talents and abilities, picking fights with those in leadership over my false sense of arrogance, and disrespecting others. At the same time, experiencing betrayal from those, I thought cared for me, being shredded to pieces by many I had come to rely on for spiritual encouragement and support.

Eventually, while neck-deep into this season in my life, my reliance on God was nonexistent; I began to experience a deep faith crisis. I did not even know who I was in God's eyes, even less in the eyes of my wife. I was so broken inside that, eventually, my unreasonable decision process led me to initiate divorce proceedings with the women I had once believed to be the one. Equally painful to me was the decision, which I then perceived as necessary at the time, to step down from my then 14 years of ministry as a Salvation Army Officer (clergy). A multiplication of poor decisions that ultimately lead me across the country, and for over five years now, I've forced to do the only real thing that any of us can do, and that is to seek God first and Him only and to trust in Him alone; that I may learn again to live in His hope.

The articulate Apostle Paul himself reminds the Christian Church in Rome that since we have been made righteous through Christ's faithfulness, we have peace with God through our LORD Jesus Christ. We have access by faith into this grace in which we stand through Him, and we boast in the hope of God's glory. But not only that! We even take pride in our problems because we know that trouble produces endurance, endurance produces character, and character produces hope. This hope doesn't put us to shame, he says, because the love of God has been poured out in our hearts through the Holy Spirit, who has been given to us (Romans 5:1-5 CEB).

When I was a young boy growing without a care in the world, little did I know that God was preparing me for a wilderness experience; I don't mean that just symbolically. I do share the name of the great desert traveler himself, Moses (more on him later); I mean, I quite literally moved to a desert when I was eleven. From beautiful Cuba right into the heart of the Southwest itself; Phoenix, Arizona. Much like with Moses' life, I can look back at those years of actual desert living and perhaps see glimpses of how God has been preparing me, even at a young age. Training for a real-life wilderness experience, one that would see me through a season in my life; where I would go through a faith crisis, a near divorce from my wife, and the need to step away from my ministry as a Salvation Army officer. A generational ministry of preaching God's Word and serving humanity's needs which continues to this day in the faithful service of my sister and cousins.

Because of the Hope of God, it's not all bad news; I can testify that so far, God has restored many things to my life. My sanity, my security in who I am in Him, my faith in His love and grace for me, and oh yes, of course, my beautiful wife and children! I am sure today that what God has been doing in me during the last decade is to guide me to seek His will and purpose daily. Even from time to time, I still experience rejection from others, uncertainty in the future, and so much more. Yet through this ongoing time of spiritual discovery, of contrite surrender to God, I believe through His Holy Spirit, God has led me to look at the lives of many men and women in Scripture. People whom I had always thought were unflawed hero's of the faith, but, as it turns out, had themselves failed to realize that like you and I, they too had their very own faith crisis, their own wilderness experience. What were the lessons available? In what practical steps did each individual applied their experiences to grow in their faith, developed a servant's heart, and recognize the blessing that God had intended all along? All this while keeping in mind that even in the storm, God is with us. He has even gone before us to prepare the way, and He alone will equip us to mature in our faith through our trials, to fulfill the future full of hope that He has in mind for each of us (Jeremiah 29:11 CEB).

If you find hope in these pages, then I pray this book will serve as a blessing to you as it has been to me to write it. At the same time, I have put it all together, always under the prayerful guidance of God's Holy Spirit in my life. I would even say I am still going through my storm somehow, but I have learned to recognize my LORD and His guidance to make me a more faithful servant in the midst of it all. This realization helps me echo the Apostle James' words of encouragement and truly see my trials with joy! This book is not meant to be read all in one sitting, but indeed one chapter at a time. I ask that you pause between each chapter and meditate on each character, their experiences, and how they may relate to your wilderness journey. The only way to move forward is to identify and deal with those things that may be holding us back from complete restoration to God's service. May I also encourage you to always give thanks to God for His goodness in your life, no matter how insignificant it may be, before moving onto the next witness of our faith!

"THE LORD's dearest one rests safely on him.
THE LORD always shields him; he rests on God's chest."

Deuteronomy 33:12 (CEB)

1

---◆·◆·◆---

ADAM

A Wilderness Experience Caused by
Willful Disobedience. The Introduction of Sin.

God said, "Let us make humanity in our image to resemble
us so that they may take charge of the fish of the sea,
the birds in the sky, the livestock, all the earth, and all
the crawling things on earth. Genesis 1:26 (CEB)

"So she took some of its fruit and ate it, and also gave
some to her husband, who was with her, and he ate it."
Genesis 3:6 (CEB)

As we seek to start at the beginning of all things, naturally, we
arrive at Adam's creation. The passage above, however,
is not merely the beginning of Adam. God already knew
Adam would be part of His plan, and God already knew that he
would one day redeem the entire human race because of Adam's
actions. In the first six letters of the Bible, what we translate as
"in the beginning" the original Hebrew meaning behind this
phrase grants us God's complete redemptive plan from the very

beginning (Berisheet - Isaiah 46:10 CEB) Think about that, even knowing Adam (humanity) would sin, God still created them! The Psalmist testifies as much in Psalm 139:13 (CEB), "you created me, my innermost parts, you knit me together while I was still in my mother's wound!" God knows us, He knows the choices we will make, and still, He chooses to create us, to love us.

One Sunday morning, as the youth pastor was teaching how God created everything, including human beings, little Josh, a child in the Kindergarten group, seemed especially interested when they told him how Eve was created out of one of Adam's ribs. Later in the week, his mother noticed him lying down as though he were ill and asked, "Josh, what is the matter?" Little Josh groaned and responded, "I have a pain in my side. I think I'm going to have a wife." From what we know, Adam certainly had a difficult life due to his poor choices.

I don't think anyone is more recognized by many leading world religions and even the secular world than Adam the first man. In fact, in Hebrew, that's precisely what Adam means, man. In the Biblical account before Jesus or the Old Testament, the Hebrew word Adam was also used to describe Mankind (Genesis 1:27 CEB); in reference to the very first man (Adam himself). Lastly, the term can also refer to a member of the human race, "a man" (Genesis 2:5 CEB). Adam would not be a stranger to difficulties. Not only because of his decisions but also because he was truly alone. When I've had disagreements with my wife, I can reach out to friends, to my sister, to my parents, maybe even an adult child. Yet Adam (and yes Eve) all they had was each other. They couldn't call their mom and go cry on her shoulder. He couldn't play golf with his buddies or do a little shopping to get their minds off their troubles. Alone meant alone. I wonder what emotional impact that solitude had on their life?

In the accounts after Jesus' time on earth or the New Testament, the word Adam (now in the Greek) is used to connect the genealogy of Jesus Himself back to the beginning of Mankind (Luke 3:38 CEB). The Apostle Paul makes the best reference to the man Adam when he reminds the reader that Adam was the representative head of humanity; now Jesus, the Christ, is the new and eternal representative for us all (1 Corinthians 15:45 CEB). Paul also connects us all to Adam by making all nations his undeniable descendants (Acts 17:26 CEB).

From the Biblical accounts of Genesis 1 and 2 (CEB), we know that God created Mankind (Adam) in His image, "both male and female he created them." Including what appears to be a second creation account, yet it is simply a more detailed description of the same creation event. It's like me saying, today I made a hamburger for dinner. Then saying, what I did was, I took two pieces of bread and cooked the meat. I added cheese and my favorite condiment and then ate it! The same account, one has additional details. Scholars go back and forth trying to explain what the word "image" means. Some claim that it refers to a supernatural representation of the Creator; after all, Adam was given authority over creation. Others say that the image relates to the fact that humans can create life with God's blessing and the help of another (a woman, of course). Yet, others explain this image to refer to the capacity that sets man apart from other animals, such as logic, morality, language, and creativity.

I tend to think that it's a bit of all combined and that, yes, it is clearly applicable to both males and females. One gender is not greater than the other when it comes to being conceived in the image of God. Man and women both carry God's perfect seal and intended creation upon them. God's blessing to this new creation is not to go and simply enjoy His design, but indeed to be fruitful and multiply. Much like a tree reproduces itself by developing seeds that ultimately grow other trees and fruit, and so forth. In essence, with humankind, their charge was to reproduce that image of God within themselves, again and again.

A continuation of life would reflect God's divine purpose - in character, actions, and spirituality.

There is also the reality that when God created Mankind, He places them in the garden, paradise. It's as if out of His celestial workshop, He invented people and then set these pieces into place. But they are not automaton pieces that do as they are simply programmed or expected. They were meant to live in a relationship with the Creator and to develop their relationships with one another. In other words, we can conclude that when we work at forging a solid relationship with God, then our relationships with each other will be equally strong.

Further still, if we look at the relationship between a man and a woman, and if their relationship with God is strong, then their marriage will be strong by definition. I only mentioned this because I have discovered this as I went through my divorce process. Yes, we both failed to care for the relationship that God had gifted us with, but worse of all, we had failed to properly care for the relationship that our Creator had long to establish with each of us individually.

Thank God that He does forgive us when we repent and confess our mistakes, our shortcomings, and He restores love and relationship. Then, maybe you are thinking, but Moy, why did God restore your marriage, but He hasn't restored mine. Why hasn't God restored my relationship with my parents, siblings, or friends? I do not claim to know the answer to that. I certainly did not think that even God would bring me back after our year-long separation, yet He surprised me as I began to put Him first in all aspects of my life.

In your case, perhaps He will restore you fully one day; maybe, for now, it's not a healthy thing to replenish to your life. I know it wasn't for me when I cried to the heavens seeking relief from my loneliness and pain. What I do know is that God has been and continues to be faithful to His children, regardless of the troubles and wrong decisions that we cause ourselves. In my case, I have come to understand that God did not cause my initial split from my wife, but my selfish actions did. I can again testify with complete assurance that He has always been close in my times of sorrow. In fact, Psalm 34:18 (CEB) tells us as much, "THE LORD is closed to the brokenhearted and saves those whose spirits are crushed. During my separation and isolation away from my wife and kids, I learned that what I needed was to use that time to humble myself before God and draw near Him. Then, He would take care of the rest, and so far He has!

This realization, in the middle of my brokenness and sadness, has led me to seek Him indeed and ask Him to "create a clean heart in me; to put a new, faithful spirit deep inside me! To ask that He might not throw me out of His presence; not take His Holy Spirit away from me. Return the joy of His salvation and sustain me with a willing heart. (Psalms 51:10-12 CEB). Am I done with this process? By no means, I am sure; I am still very much in the middle of it all; the main difference is that I am now not overtaken by hopelessness. I am actively aware of the presence and guidance of God even in reoccurring times of spiritual dryness. Why reoccurring, because I keep forgetting to stay close to the source. More on that later on.

Back to Adam, you remember the biblical history, right? On the sixth day, God created Mankind (man and woman) and gave them dominion over all things at the end of creation. They could live in Eden, which God had made for their enjoyment, eat its fruit, interact with the animals, and work the ground to some extent to get it to produce more fruit. They could eat any plant life they wanted, except for the Tree of Knowledge of Good and Evil. God even warned Adam that if he disobeyed that he would surely die. (Genesis 2:17 CEB)

Now we know that up to this point, Adam was the only one

around; God had not yet organized Eve's atoms. It isn't until Genesis 2:18 (CEB) that God foresees that it would not be a good thing for a man to be alone. The word man here is referring to the male side of humankind. You can't have humankind with just one, I suppose. What does God do then? He caused a great sleep to come over Adam, and when he wakes up, God had made a companion for him out of one of his ribs (as we heard in the early story of the little boy Josh). Then God institutes His desires for a lasting relationship between a male and a female of the species. They shall leave their parents' homes and be joined together and become one flesh. After all, from one flesh, they both came. I love my wife's perspective on this. Adam was God's first try, I mean, He did use dirt after all, but Eve, she was the improvement to humanity as God used a rib, flesh, to design her!

Life was good for these two, mangos and guavas, as far as the eyes could see. Shade, cool walks with God in the early evenings. I wonder what their conversations were about? Space and time? It had to be since baseball and football had not yet been invented! There was no need for dishwashers or toilet seats for Adam and Eve, so more than likely; this kept the arguments down between this first couple to a minimum. That is, until Eve messed it all up, right? No, not at all; Eve is not solely at fault; after all, she was not even created when God communicated the restriction over the Tree of Good and Evil to Adam.

Additionally, much like you and I, Adam had a choice. We always have a choice. Even the option to choose incorrectly, especially if it's the choice to share in his wife's poor decision, which God had taught him not to do. It was his and his alone, and he chose alright, or more precisely, he failed with his choice. He alone disobeyed God's only restriction. Don't eat from that tree! He failed as the keeper of God's commands, not because he was the man, but as I said, because Eve was not there when God gave it. He failed to grasp the severity of God's warning fully. Indeed Adam failed all of humanity and brought us all down by permitting sin to be introduced into the mix. Eve was deceived, tricked, had the wool pulled over her eyes, but Adam dove into disobedience and rebellion head-on. He willfully sinned. But is he any different than you or I and how we submit to our sin? How we blatantly invite it back into our lives in a millisecond of weakness? Forgive me, LORD, for my disobedience of Your commands and Your perpetual grace upon my life.

It's like a kid or worse, a puppy when you tell them, don't do that, and that's the same thing you find them doing? At some point in creation, Adam, as we do ourselves, certainly deceived himself into believing that he knew better than God. When his companion brought him food to eat or a choice to make from a tree that represented that which was forbidden, he consumed it; he willfully took part in it. The devil tempted them, but it was a temptation of something they already desired. What were they even doing hanging around that tree? I mean, I would have avoided that area like the plague! At least I like to think I would have. It is effortless for us to sit in judgment over their actions, think about how often we disobey God. How many times do we come to believe that we know better? How often have we failed our families or those whom we are called to care for? Perhaps too many to count. As a result, the first man and woman are banished from paradise, reportedly Eve's labor pains are increased, and Adam would now have to work hard to get the ground to produce its fruits. Thanks a lot, you guys!

And so begins Adam's literal wilderness experience. From paradise to the barren land. The consequences of his disobedience meant that Adam would live with a two-fold penalty. First, he would now have a conflict with the other side of humanity, with his flesh, his rightful companion, and second, he would have discord with the earth, the place where he came from. On top of it all, he would eventually die. Both physically and spiritually, returning to the earth as dust and living in separation from God, requiring further atonement for his actions on behalf of humanity. The

Apostle Paul writes about this to the Romans when he reminds them that "through the actions of Adam, sin entered the world and death through that same" (Romans 5:12 CEB).

As we get a little deeper into Adams wilderness experience, we see things get a little worse when two of his sons are now in conflict with each other. So much so that the proverbial apple doesn't fall far from the tree, if you will. Cain, angry at God, thinking he knew better, offers a poor sacrifice and when it is rejected, much like his dad had done when he pushed the blame for his sinful actions on the woman. Cain seeks to blame God's justified dissatisfaction with him on his brother Abel. An act that leads Cain to become the first murderer as he takes his brother's life. I'm sure that wasn't his plan; I don't think any of us plan to live lives of sin; we sort of fall into them due to our decisions and paths we take each day. Yet another sacrifice of blood on behalf of the Adam clan must now occur. More blood must be spilled. Blood is a precious thing to God, and He will not spill Cain's as a result of his selfish act. No, he, like his father, is also banished, kicked out, forced to start again on his own and work hard to establish himself, away from God's generosity.

As a father, I can only imagine what might have gone through Adam's mind. What conversation did he and Eve have that night before going to bed? Conversations that parents have all around the world, since the beginning of history. "I can't believe Cain did what he did," said Adam, "I can't believe my gentle Abel is gone," whimpered Eve. "What did we ever do to deserve this," they must have exclaimed to each other. "Why must our faithfulness towards God still be tested so?" I wonder if it even crossed their minds that this was connected to their actions. Did Cain learn disobedience and discontentment from his dad? Did Adam tell his boys stories about the garden and God's consequent actions that began to plant a seed of disapproval in Cain's heart? But what could Adam do, carry on working the ground, continue to have difficulties with his mate, and now mourn the loss of two children?

But you know it wasn't all bad news for Adam and his partner Eve. Do you remember what God does when He confronts them after He passes His judgment on them? He actually makes clothing for them from animal skin; I mean, after all, they did not have a local Walmart that God could step in and pick up a few yards of materials. No, God takes an animal's life to clothe Adam and Eve. Hear that again; God killed an animal; in other words, blood was spilled to pay for humanity's sin. God's frustration, maybe even His anger with them, had to be satisfied, just like in our case, payment or an atonement had to be made. We don't know what type of animal it was, only that it produced sufficient material to cover the newly identified shame of humanity. But in a redemptive way, this was good news, right? After all, it made Adam and Eve the first recipients of God's plan for salvation. Of His mercy and His grace. They felt the heat of God's wrath as He passes judgment down and expulsion is directed, yet they also experience, His tender care and provision, His forgiving and loving nature. I wonder if they thought about it in this way, as they mourned the loss of their children, their broken relationship, the consequences of their actions.

Eventually, God blesses Eve who's name is related to the Hebrew word for Living. God grants at least one new life in the child Seth; a new beginning, a brand new opportunity to do things correctly this time. A new hope for the future. We know that Adam lived for a long time; I wonder if he ever recovered from his sin, from the experience with his two boys? I wonder if his relationship with his lifelong partner ever got any better? As a result, did their relationship with God improve? Did they resent each other? Did they continue to blame each other? If only you had not offered me that choice, Adam, said: If only you had not taken it, replied Eve, and round and round their centuries-old argument went.

It has been my experience, in my wilderness journey, that sometimes it seems like the wilderness is never-ending and that things will never be the same again. These days we only live about 10% of the lifespan that Adam lived, yet we still walk through painful difficulties, through seemingly impossible challenges, and have we ever been tempted to think it will never stop? It's like when you eat something cold too fast and get a brain freeze! It doesn't matter how many brain freezes you have experienced before; this one is it, you will certainly die from the intense pain this time! And then in a moment, it passes, and all is normal again. Why is it that we focus so much on the present difficulty rather than on the hope ahead? Why is it that we so easily forget how God has helped us, how He has blessed others in the past? We cry, poor me, instead of proclaiming, my God will see me through it, "He will meet our every need!" (Philippians 4:19 CEB) of this I am sure!

I trust in my heart these days that what God does is not so much that He permits our trials to linger or last longer than we feel we can manage. Instead, he makes adjustments to what we thought our future is according to His design to grant us a new beginning, a different one we had never expected before. Of course, it is a better future, one that God ordains and works out of the misery and sadness we have just come through! He never leaves us, says the Scriptures, and I am glad that He never left Adam, both the first man and humankind, but continues to guide us, even during our difficulties. God always offers a way for us to stand firm, not to get us out of it, but to survive it, knowing that these difficulties will produce spiritual endurance in us and endurance will produce hope, a Godly hope for a brighter future.

How do you see yourself in the experience of Adam? Have you willfully disobeyed because you thought you knew better, or you didn't quite believe that the consequences for your actions would be as bad as the preacher said they would be? That was part of my journey of mistakes. Do you beat yourself down for the wrong choices you have made in your relationships with your kids, spouse, or even your walk with God? I believe that when the devil gets us too focused on the negative stuff, on the wrongs we have committed, it becomes very difficult for us to accept the goodness of a God that does not punish His children, no, but disciplines and corrects us because He loves us and knows what is best.

It's not a beating or a forceful submission that He is after, but honestly to get us to live in His everlasting grace, to experience His endless mercy, to turn back to Him with genuinely repentant hearts. To move into the unknown ahead, in complete obedience to His will. Yes, Adam was banished; yes, he lost his two boys due to his sin; it forever changed his relationship with his wife. Sometimes, our actions carry real painful consequences. Adam, I am sure, struggled with it all every day of his life, yet Adam lived 930 years. I am sure that he learned in the wilderness that the only way to walk is to walk with God, and that trying to go at it alone, will never produce good enough fruit, as Cain also discovered. Good enough is not enough. We must seek to exceed our own expectations so that we may please God. We may learn many lessons from Adam; if you are not familiar with his story, just read the first few chapters in Genesis and reacquaint yourself with our ancestors. Not just with Adam or even Eve, but with the beautiful redemptive love of God, the Father, our Creator!

One final thought. Do you recall what God did once He banished Adam and Eve from the garden? He placed an angel with a flaming sword to guard another important tree located in the Garden of Eden. One which God had not refused its fruit to them before, and that was the Tree of Life. You may wonder why this is so important; well, it shows God's multiplying grace. You see now that they had sentenced themselves to live under the weight of sin, God did not want them to eat of the Tree of Life and therefore have to live forever in that very sin. In a sense, the guarantee of an end could at the very least bring a release from their guilt, knowing that they would not have to live in sin forever. The promise of Heaven and eternity with God grants us this release as well.

Aside from accounts found in some apocryphal books accredited to Moses, we do not know much about Adam and Eve or even their years after their exile from paradise. Yet if human nature is any indicator, we can probably deduce that perhaps during his long existence, Adam looked back at his life, at the choices he had once made, and hopefully learned from his experience. Because of the sin of one man, all men would become sinners (Romans 5:12 CEB), yet this does not mean that Adam could not have rekindled a relationship with God. We are not told, but perhaps there was some repentance on his part, and our God of grace maybe offered him peace. How I pray, this was the case, as it provides me great hope! I like to think that in the same way that God does not give up on us, even when we mess up royally; that He eventually continued to seek Adam and through His Holy Spirit made a way for them both to return to the loving arms of His Creator.

There are many examples of metamorphosis which we find in creation that's reflect great transformation. I like to believe that God eventually transformed Adam and made him a new creature as He does in us today. Developed him from ignorance and foolishness into wisdom and grace in God. Granting him a new purpose with a new sense of hope for the unknown path ahead. You see, change will always be a personal and emotional thing, and through the process of a wilderness experience, God will make this statement a reality in each of our lives. The secret to success then is to remain near to God. If you don't want to pray, then pray anyway. You don't want to read the Bible, then read it anyways. You don't want to spend time in silence listening for God's voice, then do it anyway. You don't feel like participating in fellowship with other believers; for God's sake, go to church, join an online community, and be among other believers. It will be in this persistent perseverance that God will grant us the opportunity to choose a newness of life, a place where we can leave our failures behind and learn to excel with God's strength and not merely exist on our own.

If we could sit down with Adam and asked him for some guidelines to help us manage conflicts and loss in our lives, he might say something along the lines of: major in giving soft answers rather than harsh words. Manage what you have acquired by learning from your experiences and refusing the foolishness of life. Ultimately, marvel at the result and take it in, and as you do, find ways to spread that knowledge, that the outcome may serve as a blessing for others as well (Proverbs 15:1-12 CEB).

Jesus, you see, has accomplished these things for us; He gave His life so that we would not have to live in sin forever, separated from our Creator for all eternity. Jesus wants us to learn from His experience and apply them daily to our lives, learning to hope in Him when all hope is gone. To move forward in anticipation of His care and provision even when we cannot see it. Jesus restores, in fact, the Tree of Life, as He offers us eternal life with Him in Heaven. We still don't have to live in sin forever, but thanks to God's multiplying grace, we can live forever, in eternity with Him! Even in our wilderness experience, God is merciful. How do you need to experience His mercy today? Even now, would you kneel on the altar of your heart, as the Spirit of God has been ministering to you, and respond to God's calling in your life? He wants to redeem you; yes, He does, so come to Him! Please allow me to pray:

Father, thank you that even when we feel so far from you, you are still weaving our circumstances back into Your redemptive plan for our lives. As we see our journey in the life of Adam, help us to recognize the lessons you are bringing to our hearts. The character transformation you are producing, the perpetual and everlasting grace and love you bestow on us. Your desire was not for Adam to be lost forever or for us to perish in our sin, but that we may live for eternity with you. Redeemed, restored, and regenerated.

May it be so, may we seek Your will daily, trust in Your mercy every minute of the day and depend on Your love and desire for you always. And as we do, as you walk with us through our times of preparation, ready us to complete Your purpose. Thank you for Your restoring power; whether we have already experienced it or in faith can believe you will pour on us one day. Bless us on our journey, and may we be so ever aware of the moving of Your Holy Spirit in our lives, no matter how small His influence may feel like. For it is through His name that we pray by the redemptive blood of Jesus, amen.

Questions to keep exploring.

How does your wilderness journey relate to that of Adam? How has your uninvolved actions in your own life cost you to lose out on God's purpose and blessings?

What is your biggest temptation when God's response seems to be, wait?

What happens when you seek forgiveness from others, and such release is not granted?

Like faith, doubt can begin as the smallest of ideas that can grow into a forest confusing us; rather than a paradise of contentment. In what areas of your life do you hear such lies from the enemy, such as: Did God really say that?

As we saw in the original Hebrew, when referring to the creation of man, it refers to Mankind, including the two - God created genders. How should this inspire our understanding and actions towards equality of opportunity for both sexes?

Did Eve pick an apple, or did she choose evil? (Latin for Malum)

Why do we rarely hear mention of daughters? Plenty of these couples had them, yet only a handful from time to time make it in the pages of Scripture?

2

JOB

A Wilderness Experience Caused by the Unexpected.
A season of suffering that verifies genuine faith.

THE LORD has given, THE LORD has taken away;
bless the name of THE LORD. Job 1:21 (CEB)

No one expects God to allow the devil to afflict His children so directly, yet this was exactly what happened to Job. As we read the accounts of Job, no one could deny that Job was not happy with his wilderness experience, and undoubtedly, he complaints about it. Yet, he is able to testify in our opening verse: "THE LORD gives, THE LORD takes away, bless the name of THE LORD." (Job 1:21 CEB). And again Job proclaimed: "You gave me life and showed me kindness, and in Your providence watched over my spirit" (Job 10:12 NIV). Lastly, he concludes, "my redeemer is alive" (Job 19:25 CEB). We must come to a point in our Christian walk where we acknowledge and accept that everything that happens in this world is within the sphere of God's divine plan and or His control, a crucial part of His perfect Providence. Providence is the means of God's foresight, the way

He anticipates and prepares for our future. Providence is the way God guides and steers human history, how He teaches each one of us as He makes Himself present and active in the world, sustaining it and ruling it.

Did you know that God has a specific and unique destiny for you? Sometimes this thought may worry some of us, that we might somehow mess things up badly and miss out on God's purpose. But that isn't the case. He can even use our mistakes for good. In all circumstances of our lives and the events going on around us, we can trust in the providence of God. If we cannot arrive at this hopeful conclusion, then mourning our pain, our distress, and the darkness they reflect will consume us rather than help us grow in our faith. Scientists tell us that darkness does not exist independently but that it is merely the absence of light. The moon itself would be a dark void, an object hanging in the blackness of space if it did not reflect the light of the sun. When you and I find ourselves in the midst of a wilderness experience, things can seem pretty dark, that is until we remember to rely on the Son and ask Him to bring His light of hope into our most challenging situations.

By the way, I think I left you in the dark concerning my divorce in the previous chapter; by a miracle of God, the process was never finalized by the State. Instead, God restored my relationship with my wife, and the official divorce proceedings were eventually nullified by the Judge in charge of our case. In a liberal state such as California, where the strength of the family unit is quickly tossed aside for misguided liberal thoughts of independence and self-reliance instead of unity and commitment of a man and a woman, the divorce was just never signed off on by a Judge after almost a year in this process. Yet when God brought us back together again, and we agreed to give it another go, we submitted paperwork to cancel all proceedings. Within a couple of weeks, we had a signed order from said Judge that she had canceled all proceedings. God is truly good, and He knows how to take care of His children. Truly He weaved even my poor decisions into an experience of blessing and mercy. Yes, the enemy still tries to trip us, but we know where our hope is, and as long as we keep our eyes on Him, then no wilderness experience will ever be too unbearable again for our marital development.

At the beginning of every big boxing fight or any big major wrestling event, they usually begin with the announcer asking the question: "ARE YOU READY TO RUMBLE?" The crowd goes wild because this is why we watch; we want to see the big fight. We want to see the little guy go up against the champ or the champ beat up the presumptuous wanna-be. Now I don't know about you, but the first chapter in the book of Job has got to be the most difficult passage of Scripture I have ever read. Did God really give the devil permission to mess with Job, who was by God's testimony a righteous man? (Job 1:12 CEB). The answer is yes! It would seem that God had a preordained wilderness time for Job, and his faith is going to be pushed to the limits!!! Before we despair too much, I want to set up the events of Job's life by asking you this question: "ARE YOU READY TO RUMBLE?" The main event is about to begin, between the Almighty and a wanna-be!

Think about it for a second. Did God give Job up because Job's faith in God was weak, or because God knew that regardless of what could come Job's way, Job would remain faithful to God? It's the second reason, by the way! God knows, and Job was surely not ready to face this fight! Yet, what does this mean in practical terms? That God knows you and what you can take, so just trust in Him. If you think it's too much, if you feel you are drowning in your trials, seek the help of the lifeguard Jesus! I can't help but think, if I was in Job's sandals, would I turn away from God in the hopes of relief or persevere through my trials, believing as we have already stated that the hope of God would not only see me through it but would be with me all the way? Really think about that question. Is your response, perhaps, although an honest one, is it one that you are not too excited about? I like to think I would stay close to my God, but even the disciples deserted Jesus, right? Every single one of them ran, and unfortunately, so do I at times.

For quite some time now, I have traveled through my wilderness experience. A faith crisis, a mild depression, a darkness of the soul; call it what you will, I've experienced it. I've had good days and weeks and some bad ones as well. Along the way, I have heard it said that you should not pray for patience because God may give you a broken leg. Well, that's just cruel, isn't it, and it's not the God I serve. Instead, I have prayed for patience to endure my tribulations in faith, and God continues to lead me to the man who wrote the book on the subject, Job! If you are like me, then you may have felt abandoned at some point, as if no one cared for you. Unjustifiably, someone invented lies about your person that possibly damaged many perceived or hoped opportunities for you. Those who claimed to care for you dismissed you and forsook you or just sat in judgment over your actions. Your hundreds of friends and even family members on Facebook abandoned you, saw you as untouchable, so they quickly denied any knowledge of you, forfeited any desires to stand by you in your times of struggle. And probably worse, those that remained by your side likely only caused you more stress by questioning the reasons why you were going through such a difficult time.

I'm sure Job felt this way too; maybe in his mind, he wondered why God no longer cared for him. When Jesus Himself was on the cross and the total weight of the world's sin, past, present, and future, were deposited upon His shoulder. When the Father in Heaven could not even look at His Son because of the sin that engulfed Him, Jesus cried out, Father, why have you forsaken me? In the worst way, Jesus felt abandoned with no connection to the Father, experiencing complete separation from the source of hope, from the head of the Trinity. We do not fully share that in our Christian journey; after all, God has promised not to leave or forsake us. Yet, to our weak human hearts, any interpretation of a heavenly silence or disownment can damage us in ways we never thought possible. You see, my own experience took me from nearly losing the love of my life plus my children to being cast off from the ministry I had given my life to.

In my time of wilderness, I have done a lot of what I recognize now as useless wondering, and as a result, I have learned that life is truly a matter of perspective. Yes, during actual pain, actual abandonment, and true suffering, God's promise for His child is that He will be with them. Still, my hurt has caused me to question the validity of such a contract from time to time. And yet one thing I do know for sure, you and I are God's children, so this promise is for us! I think that maybe, just maybe, Job at some unconscious level understood this reality, this everlasting, unchanging goodness of God. Yet satan, as the book of Job calls him, stupid, selfish, and narrow-minded as he is could only think of trying to trip Job's faith up without realizing on what solid foundation Job's faith was built on.

Is the enemy of this world attempting to trip you up? On what solid foundation is your faith in God built on? Is it on a false proclamation of a god who is only a god of love, but there is no room for justice and correction? Or the other extreme, how about the false god who only cares to punish and discipline his children, but there is never any room for mercy or grace? This was the worldview of some of Job's so-called friends. In the church itself, we have continued to believe and practice these two false representations of God. He is either an angry, vengeful old man or some tree-hugging, flower child deity—the God of the Old versus the God of the New Testament.

Yet there is no such thing as the God of the Old Testament and the God of the New Testament. It is ridiculous to ever think of such a distinction. Friends, God is both just and loving and merciful and robust, and at times angry, while at other times peaceful. This doesn't mean He has some mental illness or any other type of emotional instability; after all, you and I are all those things all the time. Right? The Bible is a beautiful book that builds upon itself. One story told through the lives of dozens of faithful servants that kept God's redemptive work continuously in the forefront of humanity's existence. Think of this, the Bible that Jesus read was what we call the Old Testament. The first compilation of what we now call the New Testament books was organized around 140 AD, over 100 years after Jesus walked the earth.

So how can we come to incorporate Jesus' ministry of repentance and grace and love without fully grasping the lessons of the Hebrew Bible, the Old Testament? How does Jesus' sacrifice on our behalf make any sense, unless we study the similarities between Job and Jesus, and many other Biblical personalities? What's the meaning of the offerings God required, of the tabernacle, of his prophets? We cannot, and we must not separate the two. God was not a God of righteousness and then became a God of love. No, He has always been both; because of His righteousness, He loves us, and because He loves us, He is righteous. The lessons found in Job, and Adam and others in the Old Testament, are crucial, practical examples to help keep us all walking close to our creator. Why do I share all this? Because it is essential to understand that the same God who was allowing these perceived horrific things to take place in the life of Job is the same God who may be permitting whatever it is that you and I may be going through right now. He is the same God that allows us to go through a time of wilderness and the same God that promises to see us through it; all that it requires is that we hold on to our faith in Him.

In the Hebrew alphabet, each letter not only has its phonetic sound as we do in our English alphabet, but each character is also a symbol that carries additional meaning as well as a number that adds further understanding. The name of Job himself carries wonderful hope for us all. The meaning of his name truly is that "God the Father will accomplish a mighty deed ordained in heaven, to secure for man a heavenly home fashioned by the Son of God." (CJ Lovik - 3D Bible) He who is the author and finisher of our lives. Additionally, the Scriptures also remind us that for those who love God, He has prepared things for them that no one has seen, or ears have heard, or that have crossed the mind of humans. (1 Corinthians 2:9 CEB, Isaiah 64:4 CEB). We may see this event as a terrible no good moment in history, but God's purpose is greater than our limited understanding.

Dear friends, I do not believe God permits trouble in our lives because He gets a kick out of it, but because He knows what you and I can handle it. Furthermore, He will use that experience however it may shape out to be, to strengthen our faith and hope in Him! The Apostle Paul, who was a scholar of the Hebrew Bible, reassures us again that "no temptation has seized us that isn't common to people." (1 Corinthians 10:13 CEB). The Palmist even recognizes that "God sees our grief and He bears it with us." (Psalm 10:14 CEB). We are not a mere compilation of amino acids that happened to come together to form life; we are God's accomplishment as the Apostle Paul describes it, we were "created in Christ to do good things, things He planned out ahead of time for us to live daily." (Ephesians 2:10 CEB) I'm sorry, but your sin and temptation are not unique to you. This is why testimony times are so important because we can learn from each other's mistakes and from how God might be working His will in someone else's life.

Here is some more biblical evidence for us all. The Apostle Paul delivers again in 1 Corinthians 10:13 (CEB) when he says: "but, God is faithful!" I got to tell you, this verse is up there with John 3:16, Psalm 23, and Joshua 1:9. God is faithful. Period! This is who God is, and because He knows us better than we know ourselves, He will never permit us to be tempted beyond our capabilities; instead, Paul adds, "with the temptation God also gives us the way to endure it." However, too often, we miss it because we get consumed by our trials and temptations and forget to look for the lesson or the way out which God always provides. What is the purpose of our temptation them? We can ask Jesus about it, or we can read about it! When He was in the desert, the Scriptures tell us, he was tempted, and that like in our case, and in the case of Job, it was meant to strengthen His faith, His resolved, His commitment, and His understanding of God's faithfulness! How did Jesus find meaning? By trusting God and quoting Scripture!

We know from the book of Job that Job never cursed or gave up on Jehovah-Jireh, the provider he knew. His faith held up to such a degree that right away in chapter one of Job, our hero can proclaim in full faith, "THE LORD gave, and THE LORD takes away..." (Job 1:21-22 CEB). Wow! Can you believe that? I mean, how many times have I grown impatient with God and have lashed out at Him, have questioned Him, have doubted Him? And yet my troubles have never come up to be one-tenth of what Job lived through. Father, forgive me and help me to be more aware of Your guidance and perfectly timed plan for my life.

Some have claimed that the accounts of Job are a mere illustration, and so that's why Job can endure so much. According to how I understand this Scripture, I do not believe that Job was a fictional character. Additionally, he is mentioned by the Prophet Ezekiel and the Apostle James. He was real, and his faith was tested for reals, just like yours and mine are from time to time. Do you recall how Job's faith was tested? He was a pretty wealthy guy, a person of integrity, who feared God and avoided evil (Job 1:1 CEB). He was doing just fine, simultaneously enjoying a rewarding relationship with God and partaking in the blessings that God brings upon us as a result of our faithfulness. Great big family, a bunch of kids and servants alike, and plenty of stuff to spare! Yet, at a moment's notice, his world was turned upside down.

Have you ever received some bad news? Did you get an unexpected call, a letter in the mail, a personal messenger sharing with you something you had never imagined possible? Well, Job could tell us a thing or two about this. Let's experience it straight from Scripture.

Job 1:13-22 (CEB). "One day, Job's sons and daughters were eating and drinking wine in their oldest brother's house. A messenger came to Job and said: "The oxen were plowing, and the donkeys were grazing nearby when the Sabeans took them and killed the young men with swords. I alone escaped to tell you."

While this messenger was speaking, another arrived and said: "A raging fire fell from the sky and burned up the sheep and devoured the young men. I alone escaped to tell you."

While this messenger was speaking, another arrived and said: "Chaldeans set up three companies, raided the camels and took them, killing the young men with swords. I alone escaped to tell you."

While this messenger was speaking, another arrived and said: "Your sons and your daughters were eating and drinking wine in their oldest brother's house when a strong wind came from the desert and struck the four corners of the house. It fell upon the young people, and they died. I alone escaped to tell you." Job arose, tore his clothes, shaved his head, fell to the ground, and worshipped."

How much bad news can one person take? How much can you and I take before we turn away from God and go try to make sense of it all on our strength? Job never did abandon his faith, as confirmed in the Scriptures, when we find him worshipping upon receiving such a plethora of terrible news. How can we, like Job, find the spiritual, emotional, and maturing success that he experienced? We must understand the "why" of why we are tempted. Phillip Yancey talks about this in his book, The Bible that Jesus Read, and he says that "is by always recognizing that any attacks of the enemy will always carry these three perspectives and lies.

- When the temptation comes our way, it is always an attack on God's Character.
- When we are tempted, we are expected to believe that God is not worthy of love.
- Lastly, the enemy would have us believe that people follow God only because they think they will get something out of it."

First of all, the devil will always try to attack God's Holy and righteous character. Introduce doubt in our minds and so turn us away from Him. Doubt is like faith; just a little bit can make a significant impact! Yet, never forget my brothers and sisters that God is sovereign in all things. Nothing rules Him, but everything is His! David Proclaims in Psalm 24:1 (CEB), "the earth is the Lords and everything in it, the world and its inhabitants too." Never doubt God's faithful Character, He never doubts yours. But I thought my temptation was all about me? No, the enemy is trying to discredit our perfect heavenly Father through our reactions to his tricks. Does that mean that if I don't live up to God's plan, does the devil make God a liar? Absolutely not; even when we fail, God's faithfulness and untarnished reputation prevail. He remains with us and ultimately restores us.

Secondly, the enemy wants us to think that God does not deserve our love because God doesn't work in our timing. He doesn't get us out of our trouble or heal our sick family members, restore our marriages, bring us joy again when we want it. In Job, we see that the devil has access to God, but don't be mislead; he is not God, not even close. Satan may be free to go around the earth, but he knows nothing about our loving heavenly Father who disciplines those He loves or a merciful God who gives His only Son as a sacrifice for the sins of humankind. Don't believe the enemy or anyone else that may try to convince you otherwise. God indeed is love, and we can love one another because God first loved us! (1 John 4:19 CEB). Therefore, even through our times of wilderness, God wants to show us how much He cares for us through the work of grace of the Holy Spirit so that we may then care for others as they go through similar situations.

And lastly, the enemy would have you think that we only love God because we expect something in return. Yet, Moses spent 40 years in his wilderness experience. David waited almost two decades to take his place as the rightful king while a crazy king pursued him. Job lost everything in what seemed like an instant. Yet, they all remained faithful to God. Not because they would get anything out of it, but because they knew God is the only place of hope, especially when going through tribulations. More on each of those servants later on.

When satan came to present himself before God, he claimed that God had a protection around Job! Thank God that He does protect His children. But then God surprises him by saying, ok, give it a try, and you will see how genuine Job's faith in me is. Yes, God watches over us, yes God allows temptation to come our way, and yes, God wants us to be good and succeed in spite of our trials like we tell our children. Yet there is nothing we can do to earn His mercy or to deserve His amazing grace, it is all unmerited, and God gives it freely to an undeserving race, you and me, why? Because He so loves us so!

Whenever you are tempted, or life gives you more than you feel you can handle, remember these things and know that you are amid temptation, and the first thing you should do is drop to your knees and seek God's help. He will help you! Believe it, friend. Jesus did, and so did Job, and God worked it out for good! (Romans 8:28 CEB). God is truly working in your life. Max Lucado wrote: "A season of suffering is a small assignment when compared to the reward. Rather than begrudge your problem, explore it. Ponder it. And most of all, use it. Use it to the glory of God."

Now, did you know the story of Job is not really about Job or even about suffering? I know when you read it, you will think I am crazy; after all, most of the book is around the very suffering of Job, yet that's not what it is about. I believe that Job's accounts are really about humanity's faith or our ability to have faith in our creator. God believes in Job, so much so that He permits terrible things to come his way, to prove to the enemy that humanity's faith in God can be genuine. With Adam and Eve, the devil got them to doubt God's provision for them. Yet with Job, he failed! We too must relate to this because we often come to put God on trial when we suffer or when life happens around us in ways we feel we did not deserve. So does our faith hold? Do we sin against God in our despair, maybe because we don't understand why it is happening, or do we hold on strong against all odds and praise the name of THE LORD for it?

As a result, we must ask, is there a good reason for suffering, or is it just life happening? After all, the sun shines, and the rain falls on the righteous and the unrighteousness alike, still even the sun and the rain have a good purpose, to bring life and growth. The answer then is yes and yes! Sometimes stuff does happen, but can you believe that God can use the worse of incidents for good? Viktor Frankl, a survivor of a Nazi concentration camp, concluded that "the worst despair is suffering without meaning." In the middle of your trials, are you asking God not just to get you out but to show you what the lesson is? Perhaps seeking what spiritual truth, what character purification He has in mind for you, what change He desires for you to undertake, or even what faithful attribute He intends to fortify in you?

As the Apostle James proclaims, if we consider our troubles as joy, we can know with full assurance that it will produce spiritual endurance in us, and like a seasoned athlete, we will become mature, we will find hope for the things to come! (James 1:2-4 CEB). We gain great insight when we allow our perception of our pain to be used to build up our faith rather than tear it down. Hellen Keller, who was blind and death was an American author who said: "character cannot be developed in ease and quiet. Only through experience of trial and suffering can the soul be strengthened, ambition inspired, and success achieved." Do we look at pain as a bad thing or as an opportunity to show the enemy who we truly trust in our lives! A real opportunity to grow in our walk with God?

Dear reader, I know it's not easy; I mean, even Jesus called out, "my God, why have you left me all alone," quoting King David in Psalm 22 (CEB). I am sorry, but the pain will come, and pain will go; good people do suffer, and bad people sometimes seem to get away with it. Bosses sometimes treat their employees as less than human, and sometimes this also happens in church settings. The pettiness of humanity can sometimes cause the holiest of believers to treat the less Holy ones as inferior and, therefore, as dispensable. But God loves you and is preparing you for an eternity with Him. So hold on, the wait will be worth it! For this reason, Jesus Himself proclaims in John 16:33 (CEB), "in this world, you will have trouble, but be encouraged, for I have the world! (More on Jesus later) The story of Job does have a happy ending if you will. The rumble is concluded by Job's faith in God holding and then God humiliating the enemy by indeed proving the genuineness of humanity's faith in Him.

Job makes it through the wilderness, and then we get Job's confession to God; yes, this is part of the road we must take through our trials and circumstances. Job confesses his lack of understanding in God's ultimate will and even his unwillingness to be open to God's instruction (Job 42 CEB). Yet, in the middle of it all, Job is still able to proclaim that His savior, His redeemer is alive and that in the end, He will stand. Regardless of Job's situation, he understood that God's purpose for him included his ultimate salvation. Not just a redemption at the end of time, but an immediate and present salvation as well. The Apostle Paul confirms as much when he reminds his disciple Timothy that "God has saved us and call us into a Holy calling." (2 Timothy 1:9 CEB) It's in the past tense. Saved, meaning it has already been completed and done so, so that we may be able to live Holy lives as He actively calls us to live Christlike lives every day from now on. As a result of this salvation, ultimately, God fully restores Job's health, his family, and his possessions.

I pose to you, my friends, that we grow impatient and angry with God when we go through the wilderness, through dry seasons, through desert experiences because we may not understand God's will or be resistant to His teachings. Whatever you may be going through today, may I encourage you to put your guard down, stop defending yourself against God and simply submit to Him? Confess your sin, your wrongdoings, your shortcomings, and ask God not only to forgive you but to teach you and to guide you. Ask Him to show you the best way that He may be glorified in your life, especially in your trials and temptations, of which I am sure He has permitted to come your way because just like with Job, He knows your faith in Him is genuine! Are you feeling tempted or like me going through trials? Then draw near to God and ask him to strengthen your trust in Him!

I've come to the point in my journey so far where I've started to think like Job especially relating to my marriage; God gives, and He takes away. How else could it be that while I was praying for reconciliation with my wife, she was praying for release because of the deep hurts we had caused each other? And yet He answered both our prayers in reverse. He granted me release from what I thought I needed and simply got me to a place where I learned to trust in Him more. And with my wife, He showed her the purity of His intention for a man and a woman, and through many conversations together and much forgiveness, He reconciled us back together. God who had given us to each other permitted a temporary separation before we damaged His image in each other too terribly. And you know what, we learned for a time to be ok with that. That is, we were willing to let each other go for the sake of a closer walk with God. At least in my case, I learned to hold onto Job's words when he said, God is faithful, meaning He knows better than I do what is best for me.

One of the main things I have learned from my experience so far has been not to ask God to get me out of my situation. That's easy; that's what we all want, so I am convinced that God is aware of this; after all, He does not permit these things merely to see us suffer through them unnecessarily. But what I believe God has done is show me what I am supposed to change, learn or do differently. To seek His Spirit's help, to be still, to listen, yes I dare even say to slow down. With God's help, I have been able to learn to trade in my sorrows, as the song says, even if it meant that I might never get my family back, that I might never get my ministry back. But remember, God is always faithful, and in His time, He has restored most things. Those He knows I can manage right now! Others still to come, so I'll keep hoping!

As Job would testify, the wilderness experience is a crucial part of our holiness journey, which is often an ongoing development of our Christlike character. But not just for us, but so that through our struggles, others may come to know the love and mercy of God (Romans 14:8 CEB); after all, we are the salt of the earth, bringing the right amount of God flavor to a tasteless world. We did not mention Job's so-called friends too much in this lesson. Yet, they were ruthless in their interpretation of Job's condition. They only made his wilderness experience all the worse. They critiqued Job, blames Job, made him feel less than human. Yet, in the end, they too experienced God's mercy as a result of Job's prayer on their behalf. Wait, so you telling me wilderness experience will also include forgiveness? Not include it, but be one of its primary purposes. Without forgiveness, there can't be healing. Without forgiveness, there can't be hope for the future. Without forgiveness, there is no growth in our Christian journey.

Our LORD Jesus reminds us that before restoration can begin in us, we must be willing to restore others! "Therefore, if you bring your gift to the altar and there remember that your brother or sister has something against you, leave your gift at the altar and go. First, make things right with your brother or sister and then come back and offer your gift." (Matthew 5:23-24 CEB) The gift that we can bring to God is our obedience, our respect; it's our surrender. Yet if we remember someone who may be indebted to us, we must go and restore them first, make things right with them as much as possible, then return to offer our offering to God.

Who do you need to make amends with today? What must you simply release, just let go, to trust that God has you and He will take care of your situation? At the end of his ordeal, Job was able to testify of God, "I know that you can do anything; no plan of yours can be opposed successfully." (Job 42:2 CEB) God has a plan for you, and nothing anyone can do can stop him from loving you and seeing it to fruition. Just get to know God in your time of struggle that your faith in Him may be confirmed. (Job 42:5 CEB) There is one sure thing we can all do; we can pray and seek His purpose together, that we may be a vessel of influence for those going through similar struggles as we may be.

Here are some ways I would think Job would encourage us to influence others into faith and hope in God rather than do what our culture seems to keep doing, destroying each other. (1) Nurture not frustrate. (2) Care don't dismiss. (3) Be optimistic, not negative. (4) Love not denigrate. (5) Respect not minimize. (6) Encourage, not intimidate. (7) Boost not hinder. You give it a try!

Father, we admit that we do not always understand Your will, and in our frustration, as a result of the trials and temptations that come our way, we may turn from you, making things worse. Forgive us when we don't understand, forgive us when our faith is weak, but for this, we pray, help our unbelief, help us to be attentive to the moving of Your Spirit in our lives so that as temptation comes our way, we may indeed count them joy. Knowing that you are with us, knowing that you are working through us, strengthening us, and preparing us for higher service in Your Kingdom.

LORD, we humble ourselves today in Jesus' name; we put our guard down and surrender fully to you. Accept our sacrifice of self and speak to our hearts this day we pray. Thank you for the lesson of hope found in the story of Job, a hope that reminds us that you believe in us, that you know what we are capable of, and instead of operating on our strengths, all that you ask is that we lean on you, that we trust you. It is my confession this day, Father, that I will do just that, as you help me, as you guide me, as you strengthen me, for Your honor and glory.

Questions to keep exploring.

It would seem that the devil not only had access to God, but God permitted him to inflict pain on Job. How was he able to do this? Did he still have access to the hearts and minds of other people? (Think of what the four messengers came to report to Job)

If Job was such a man of God, why did God have to prove anything to the devil? Why grant such an evil request?

How do you perceive the work of God's Holy Spirit in your life for your benefit as a result of what he may be allowing you to go through?

When God restored Job's children to Him, do you think he granted him brand new babies, or were his sons and daughters brought back to life?

A potentially dangerous question to explore would be, why do the Righteous suffer? Why does God allow it?

Have you been able to identify your trial's why or, better yet, how have you seen God use your experiences to minister and encourage others?

3

———◆•◆———

JOSEPH

A Wilderness Experience Brought Upon Arrogance.
A season of suffering meant to bless others.

"But Joseph said to them, "Don't be afraid... You planned
something bad for me, but God produced something
good from it in order to save the lives of many people."
Genesis 50:19-20 CEB

Have you ever heard the expression, if you are in a hole, stop digging? The early days in the life of Joseph often make me think about this saying. He was number 11 out of 12 brothers, all sons of Jacob (who had his name changed to Israel by God). I can only imagine that being born in such a lowly position in the family pecking order can make it difficult for a person to search for attention, for acceptance, even for identity; it must have been a constant battle for Joseph. However, we have all known a "little brother" who has allowed their zeal to carry them away. With extravagant stunts, usually being a bit anxious and loud, they sought to be the center of attention. Joseph, you could say was no different.

As we read through his story, it becomes clear that young Joseph brings upon himself the wrath of his brothers, which will set him on a difficult path. In my wilderness experience, I cannot avoid the fact that I believe I have caused or set in motion many of its components because of the way that I had often chosen to react to situations. Some may even say overreact! Much like in Joseph's early days through my arrogance, selfishness, mistake after mistake that did not add up to anything good.

Joseph sure dug a literal hole for himself, which he could not get himself out of no matter what he did. Maybe you can relate to this as well. At one point, we read that his brothers throw him into a physical hole as they plotted their revenge on his life. However, we have to admit it's not entirely Joseph's fault that he is so excited about what God is sharing with him. How many of us have not gotten into some sort of trouble with our supervisors before? When we put the cart before the horse, getting ahead of ourselves and making claims that others were not ready to accept yet? No one? Ok, then it's maybe just me!

If you are not familiar with the story of Joseph, he had received a series of dreams from God concerning his future, and not knowing how to interpret them correctly quite yet, he blurred them out to his already frustrated gang of brothers. Additionally, we know from the accounts of Joseph's life that he was, we could say a bit of a tattle tell. Yes, he would go to work with his elder brothers and tell dad about their misbehavior. You can imagine how this made him very popular with them! I remember occasions when I felt frustrated by someone, and I would run to tell of their perceived injustices to those I felt could do something about it. Yet, it only served to push would-be saviors away and create a reputation for myself that would grant me no mercy later on when I truly needed it, how I regret those actions terribly.

Joseph's father doesn't help much either when he makes a classic mistake that, of course, does not benefit the situation either. If you have at least two children of your own, you know that you are not supposed to have favorites. I mean, you can think you like one more than the other, or believe one is more talented or street smart than the other; however, you don't tell them, wait, really? I guess only me again, right, right! Out of Israel's twelve sons, Joseph is number 11, and Benjamin, number 12, and they were the sons of his beloved Rachel. She was Israel's wife, the one he had worked for almost 20 years for, the one his family had set aside for him. These were also the children of his old age, you could say. Israel loved Joseph so much that he did not care to publicly show his love for him by giving him a beautiful multicolor coat.

Of course, there is nothing wrong with showing your love to your children, but in this case, the Bible tells us that when Israel did this that Joseph's brothers hated him and could not speak a kind word to him. Yikes, there goes that popularity meter again, down and down it goes. Is there something you have done in your life that has caused others to hate you, not want to address you even if you are standing in the same room? I have, I don't say that with pride but, with regret, with contrition and remorse, even though some of the worse things I was accused of were invented lies. However, I have seen many of the choices I make while away from God often bring consequences to me and hurt others. I am not just talking about family, although they are our first casualties in our selfish actions. But I'm talking about the world around us. Our coworkers, our bosses, those who are in stewardship over us. Dr. Sandra Wilson wrote a book about this, called "Hurt People, Hurt People." An eye-opening read.

Remember the story of the prodigal son? His selfish acts ultimately caused him great distress, but they also affected his household, his father, and his brother. Make no mistakes about it; when we walk away from God's will is not just us who are affected, the collateral damage we leave in our wake can be measured by the disapproval and even hatred that our actions cultivate in the hearts of others. By this point in his life, Joseph is not liked by his brothers very much. Indeed, only his mother and father seem to care for the kid. Enter God's dreams. God gives Joseph a dream where Joseph and his brothers were in a field bindings sheaves of grain, and all of a sudden, Joseph's sheave rose higher than the others, and those representing his brothers gathered around him and bowed to him. Undoubtedly, Joseph is encouraged by this revelation, makes a tactical mistake, and shares this dream with his brothers. Did they embrace him and thank God for him? Think again; the scriptures are clear that his brother's response was not a good one. "You intend to rule us?" they proclaimed. And then the scripture says that they hated him even more because of it. Not looking good for little Joe, is it?

Remember the illustration of digging yourself a hole? Joseph eventually has another similar dream, but now two additional sheaves, representing the sun and the moon (possibly meaning his parents), also bow down before him. Joseph thought it would be a good idea to share the second dream with his dad. Daddy, you love me right, you think I'm great, right? Check this out I had a dream, and you and mom, plus all of my knucklehead brothers, will one day bow before me. Isn't it great, father? Not so much, son, not so much. Scripture points out that his father kept the matter in mind because it bothered him so much, and his brothers, well, the Word of God, says that now they were jealous of him. Hmmm, anger, hate, jealousy, I think something good is about to come from this, think again!

If you haven't read the story of Joseph in some time, let me remind you of what happens next. In short, Joseph's self endured wilderness experience is about to get launched. As the brothers were out grassing the sheep, enjoying life, they conspired to kill Joseph. I asked earlier if your actions had ever led someone to dislike you but to want to kill you? Perhaps not physically, but maybe someone conspired to destroy your reputation, to block any opportunity for advancement, to ensure, as they say in the movies, that you would never work in this town again. And yet I, too, have gone through that, my action and lack of practical wisdom being responsible for someone else's perpetual sin and unfair judgment against me.

Joseph went out to the fields one day, showcasing his multicolor coat, probably feeling pretty good about himself after those awesome dreams, and finds his brothers not doing their jobs, and he threatens to expose them to their father. This kid just doesn't learn, does he? And the brothers jumped into panic mode. If it weren't for the delay of his eldest brother Ruben, who convinced the angry, jealous-filled brothers to throw him in a pit for a while, Joseph surely would have been dead on the spot. But Joseph is not out of the woods yet. Finding himself now in a literal hole, knowing that he will surely be killed when they took him out, what can Joseph do? What would you do? When the time came to put an end to this very self-assured young man, God provided for Joseph in a way that we may not think of as God's providence.

You see, a band of traders passed by, and now Judah, another one of his brothers, convinced the mob to simply sell Joseph as a slave and then created a back story for their dad, where they would claim a wild beast killed Joseph. They all agree, and Joseph is off to Egypt to begin his new life of adventure while all their troubles are done. (Not really, we call that sarcasm, in case you are wondering). I have come to believe that sometimes by the actions of others, we can be thrusted into the wilderness. Sometimes, however, we bring it upon ourselves altogether by making wrong choices, or poor ones at a minimum. Yet we must never doubt that God is able to use any situation to get us back on track, to prepare us for something new, to encourage us to seek His faithfulness constantly. It may be a quick turnaround, or it may be a matter of a longer game, but God is always faithful, and He will never forsake His children, even when they make stupid mistakes!

Joseph's self-imposed troubles are merely beginning. However, things will get worse from now on. It won't be by his doing anymore. Still, now by the circumstances surrounding this very deep metaphorical hole, he began to dig for himself a while back as he thoroughly enjoyed his egotistical life stile as daddy's favorite! Often in our journey, as we embrace complacency, we lose track of God's absolute goodness when we begin to live our lives based on the what-if question. What if God has forgotten about me, what if I am not longer His servant, what if God is mad with me and has simply dropped me, what if I have disqualified myself from His service? Instead of merely seeking, holding on, and believing His promises. When we first read about God's promises, we tend to accept them. He would never abandon us (Deuteronomy 31:6 CEB), He has plans for us (Jeremiah 29:11 CEB), God will meet our every need (Philippians 4:19 CEB). These were easy for us to believe because our faith had not yet been adequately tested.

Enter the wilderness experience, a time of spiritual contemplation, an actual time of brokenness, where the only natural choice is to hold on to whatever faith we may have and believe God's promises again rather than wander around aimlessly. Trust me; I lived in this state for some time; not fun, yet I still tried to hold on to hope even if it was just a smidgen of it. I saw Joyce Meyers a long time ago say in a televised message, "We must live by what we know and not by what we think." Faith tells us that no matter what we may be going through, God is always good, He is always graceful, He is always faithful (Isaiah 30:18 CEB, 1 Peter 5:10 CEB), so even if we are called to suffer, God will see us through it, and our commitment to Him will be the better for it. When we live our lives knowing that God has been faithful in the past to us, it certainly means that He will be faithful today and in the future, then we set ourselves up for spiritual success. A success that will produce hope, especially when we are living in great physical, emotional or spiritual need.

After Joseph is sold as a slave to Señor Potiphar's house, an Egyptian official, things soon begin to look up in our story. Well, only for a time. The Bible tells us that in spite of all that Joseph has already gone through that the Lord was with Him (Genesis 39:2 CEB). You see, in spite of his previous actions and current situations, Joseph had been taught about the faithfulness of God towards his great grandfather Abraham, his grandfather Isaac and Jacob or Israel, who was his dad. I believe that because of this knowledge, Joseph does his best to hold on to those promises that I'm sure his father shared with him while growing up. There is a clear promise in scripture from God to each of us that He will never leave us, nor forsake us, that He goes before us and prepares the way. God gave these promises to Moses and Joshua later on in the biblical account many years after the events of Joseph when God's people were being freed from Egypt and were about to enter the unknown of the Promised Land.

This, however, is the same promise that God gave to the Patriarchs of the faith when He spoke to them about making them a great nation. The promise is simple, no matter what, I am with you, I will help you, I will bless you, says the Lord. Memorize it, and it will serve as a source of hope every day of your life. Think of this as you ponder about your own wilderness experience, and rest assured that even though you may find yourself in a hole under the prospect of death, God has your back! Even if you are forced into some sort of slavery to a foreign land, being forced out of your routines, and finding yourself at the mercy of others, that God is always with you, if you remain close to Him, He will surely make you thrive one day again!

This is a promise that Jesus Himself verified later on in John 15 when He reminded us that God is the vine and we are the branches, and if we remain close to Him if we abide in His will and purpose that then and only then will we produce excellent and lasting fruit, and God will be with us. In the movies Star Wars, they love to say, "Never Underestimate the Power of the Force."

Friend, I know that in your brokenness as I have experienced in my own, it is sometimes easier just to think God has abandoned us, that He is done with us. Still, He has not, He has a plan, and even in the midst of your pain and sorrow, God will work all things together for good for the ones who love Him, for those called according to His purpose. (Romans 8:28 CEB) Never then underestimate the power of God to fulfill His promises in you. Trust that His force of grace and love and hope and kindness will follow you every day of your life (Psalm 23 CEB).

Sure, it may take some time, it may take some painful situations, it certainly cost Joseph plenty of grief as he is not entirely done yet enduring misery for the sake of God's ultimate plan. Yet Joseph appears to remain faithful to God no matter what. We see a noticeable development in his character, a growth caused by his experiences, as he relies more and more on God as his source of help and strength. The Psalmist David wrote about this up and down in the Psalms. In Psalm 31:1 CEB he proclaims, in you LORD, I take refuge. In Psalm 33 (CEB), he sings, the Word of the LORD is right and true; He is faithful in all He does. In Psalm 34 (CEB), he confesses that he sought the LORD, and He answered him; He delivered him from all of his fears. And so on and on! I have also understood that our wilderness experiences are intensified when we allow fear of the unknown to take the better of us. If you have lost your family or job or a friendship, you may come to fear that things will never be the same again and that fear will drive you into a deeper depression, yet God always remains faithful, dear reader.

Even so, Joseph, who by now is no longer the same trouble maker youth we met once, will now experience further persecution and trials even as he attempts to do the right thing. Must it be a punishment from God on him? As a direct consequence of his past actions, and now they are finally catching up to him? No, you see, God is continuing to position Joseph right where He needs him to be so that one day Joseph will have the most significant impact in the kingdom of God that he can. I believe that God is doing the same thing with you and me. You may want to be president of a nation or general of Armies or a Captain of Industries. Yet, God has you as a humble janitor, or even a school teacher, a retail associate, a drive-through attendant at the local Wendy's. Though human eyes place little value in these essential positions, God does, for He is not punishing us or holding us back. He is preparing us right where we are at for the blessings and purposes He has in store for us and others through us. Let that statement sink in a bit and rejoice in the graciousness of our father in heaven.

Times of spiritual deficiency can be perceived by the person living through it as a terrible never-ending season, but that's all they are, seasons. You guessed it, seasons come and seasons go. Seasons that bring us through to a better place, a God-ordained place, if we learn daily to seek Him and trust in His will no matter what, knowing He will take care of our situation. One day, Joseph was minding his own business and doing his job when Potipher's wife began to seduce him. I don't know about you, but this is a difficult situation for most men to find themselves in the middle of. Suppose we are honest, and I hope to be with you, for many of us to see ourselves in a situation where a powerful and beautiful woman (or man in the case of our women readers) is making advances on us. In that case, we might find it quite difficult to resist, even to justify inappropriate behavior. Yet thank God that Joseph resisted. Not only does he resist, but he physically runs away. Joseph shows us with great practical wisdom that if you are about to fall into a situation that will bring you shame or dishonor and just real difficulties in life, your job is not to play it out or see where it leads. The response of the alert Christian is not to think I can handle this; I won't give in, NO, your job, my job is to run away in the opposite direction of sin, as fast as our legs will take us.

Yet, in spite of Joseph's attempt to remove himself from this terrible situation, Potipher's wife lies about what happened. Potipher had no choice but to throw Joseph in prison, even though he may have known in his heart that Joseph was not at fault. Do not despair; it's ok, you see, for God needed Joseph to be in prison. What? How can that be? Well, it is from his prison cell that he will once again gain favor from others in leadership, and it is in this place of incarceration that he will meet two servants of the Pharaoh, and as he interprets their dreams for them, Joseph's future begins to look up. Well, not until he spends a couple of years stuck in another hole! Practical wisdom grows out of times of solitude and contemplation; in times of perceived hopelessness, God grants us opportunities to believe in the impossible. And God always delivers!

Now we can begin to see the way out of Joseph's wilderness experience as one day, still, unbeknownst to Joseph, of course, the Pharaoh himself begins to have dreams that no one else could interpret. Yet one of those servants we mentioned before, one whom Joseph had helped in prison all those years back, remembers him, and Joseph is brought before the Pharaoh to interpret his disturbing dreams. Fast forward a bit, and upon a successful interpretation of an upcoming drought in the land, Joseph is elevated in the kingdom of Egypt to only second below the Pharaoh himself. Talk about restoration! Our pal Joseph is now given significant responsibilities and put in charge of the preparations for the upcoming famine that will soon be upon the land, as Joseph correctly interpreted from the Pharaoh's dream of this impending future.

When people in power over you bully you and trust me, I still have several of those over me, trust that God still has a plan for you. He will come through to bless and help others through your continual faithfulness. It may not be in your timing; in fact, I guarantee it won't be, and that may frustrate you, maybe cause you to doubt that God honestly does care, but don't allow all of those negative voices to blind you to the amazing Grace of God. Simply keep desiring Him first, focus on His Kingdom first, and He will take care of all other things. (Matthew 6:33 CEB). That is

God's promise to you and me after all, and He always keeps His promises! Even amid my own wilderness experience, I confess to you this to be true. Joy does come in the morning, and God is with us through the night!

In the case of Joseph, after seven long years of reserving grains, a great famine fell on the land. So much so that far away, a man named Israel heard that there was food to be bought in the land of Egypt and sends his ten eldest sons down to buy some. You remember these guys right? They are the ones that basically got away with murder? They are the ones who created an elaborate story about their brother's death but pocketed the profit from selling him as a slave. They are the ones that caused their father great sorrow with the made-up events surrounding Joseph's ultimate demise. Now they are on a journey down to Egypt to the official responsible for selling food in the name of Pharaoh. Unbeknown to them, right into Joseph's hand!

I can only imagine the satisfaction that Joseph must have felt when he first saw his brothers needing his help, and he must have plotted to get back at them, to toss them into prison, to ridicule and abuse them as they had done with him. Remember, this is not the same young man we met earlier in the story. The difficulties he has faced have made him a wiser man, with a stronger character and a true sense of understanding of God's care and provision in his own life. Our human tendencies you see are to feel anxious and to worry during our difficulties. To doubt and to lose hope. To get revenge and make others pay for how they have hurt us. Yet God's Word reminds us to do the opposite. The Apostle Paul reminds the Philippians and ourselves to: "Not be anxious about anything; rather, bring up all of our requests to God in our prayers and petitions, along with giving thanks." (Philippians 4:6 CEB)

All that time we spend worrying and crying about our situation could be better spent seeking God and trying to understand

His purpose behind our suffering. Whether we brought it upon ourselves or others are intentionally hurting us. Friends, I know, trust me, I am an expert at this. When the destruction of my life was but a sure thing, I wasted months feeling sorry for myself, blaming anyone and everyone. You see, whining and pushing blame comes much easier to us, yet God is faithful, and He has a plan. Yes, He does! The Apostle Peter reminds us this time in his first letter that if we are faithful, meaning if we endure steadfastly doing good for the glory of God; yet, we are called to suffer along the way, the only option is to carry on, patiently persevering, for this behavior is pleasing to God. (1 Peter 2:20 CEB)

The enemy will try to confuse us, he will twist God's promises, yet in the end, Peter reminds us again to resist the enemy as we stand firm in our faith in God. Knowing that our fellow believers are also ensuring the same suffering. Then, Peter shares extraordinary practical wisdom with us: "After you have suffered for a little while, the God of all grace, the one who called you into His eternal glory in Christ Jesus, will Himself restore, empower, strengthen, and establish you." (1 Peter 5:10 CEB). This is precisely what God is doing in the life of Joseph, and as I look at my own wilderness journey, I can see that it is something God is actively doing in my life as well, as I learn to live my life more and more according to what pleases Him and not my own selfishness.!

We could write an entire book on what pleases God as the Scriptures are very clear on the subject. Hebrews 11:6 CEB tells us that having faith and seeking His will pleases the LORD. Romans 12:1 CEB, we read that dedicating ourselves and offering our bodies as a living and holy sacrifice will please God. If we plant Spiritual fruit in our lives and the lives of others, the fruits produced will be pleasing to our Heavenly Father (Galatians 5:22-23, 6:8 CEB). If we are faithful in preaching and explaining God's Word, this behavior will be found pleasing by God. When we speak as God leads us, He who tests our motives and knows our hearts will be pleased. (1 Thessalonians 2:4 CEB). Loving one another and treating each other as brothers and sisters in Christ will be pleasing to the Lord. (1 Thessalonians 4:9 CEB) and so on and on.

As faithful imitators of Christ, we have to do what pleases THE LORD. God is the vine, and we are His branches; if we do what He commands us, then we are truly His friends. (John 15:14 CEB). We are truly living in His will. How does God demonstrate His friendship with us? By reminding us that no one has greater love than to give up one's life for one's friend (John 15:13 CEB). This is precisely what Jesus did on behalf of those who put their faith in Him daily! Ultimately, as you read through the rest of Joseph's story in the final chapters of the book of Genesis, Joseph forgives his brothers and blesses them by giving them food. What a beautiful transformation we see in Joseph's life. Through his direct actions, the Pharaoh himself welcomes his entire family to relocate to one of the best areas in Egypt. Forgiveness, Faithfulness, and Faith will end up being the keys to Joseph's restoration and to His success as it will be for us as well!

God restores Joseph to his father Israel and, through his suffering and service, ensures that His promises to Abraham, Isaac, and Jacob (Israel, who was Joseph's father) will stand true. It will be Joseph's two sons that will, later on, become the remaining number for the twelve tribes of Judah since the tribe of Levi will one day be given ministerial and priestly responsibilities. Out of the all-important 12 tribes of Israel, Joseph, through his children, is given the privilege to father two tribes! (Manasseh and Ephraim) No matter what we are going through, if we can learn to believe that God knows best and that ultimately, no matter what we may be going through, whether it lasts for a week, a month, a year, or a decade that He is working it out for good as we remain faithful to Him.

Regardless of all that Joseph went through, whether self-imposed through his arrogance as a young man or by the doing of others, he eventually came to a place in his life where he boldly proclaimed to his brothers: "You planned something bad for me, but God produced something good from it, in order to save the lives of many people, just as he's doing today." (Genesis 50:20 CEB). Friends, never compare your weaknesses with someone else's strength. It is always easier to focus on what we lack, on the troubles we are facing, that we forget sometimes we bring them upon ourselves, through our poor choices. It is easier you seek to blame others and never look inward at our own actions or missteps. Keep your eyes instead on the faithfulness of God. One last thing, Joseph's story has a happy ending, you could say. In Genesis 45:1-7 (CEB), we are witnesses to a remarkable reconstruction in the life of Joseph. A graceful presentation of the new character that God has developed in his life resulting from his wilderness journey. A shift brought about through the threats of death from his jealous brothers, being sold into slavery, sent to an unknown country, falsely accused of a crime he did not commit, and spending some hard time in prison.

When it's time for the final reveal with his brothers, Joseph is a new man, a better man. He does not condemn them for what they did to him; he does not pray that God would teach them to listen and make them suffer as he had suffered. No instead, Joseph, with what I can only imagine was a tearful tender voice, says to his brothers; don't be distress, do not be angry with yourselves for what you have put me through because it was to save lives that God sent me ahead of you. Have you ever wondered if perhaps your wilderness experienced is meant to create in you, Godly character, but most importantly, to bless others? Surely, this was the case with Joseph! God means it all for his good! Why, because aside from what Joseph suffered, the many storms he merely survived in his journey, God was always with him, showing him grace, mercy, and favor. And you know what, I believe He wants to do the same with you and me!

A few years ago, I found myself walking on the beach, and as I began my walk, I remember praying and saying, LORD, please come and walk with me. As I walked near the water, a lite shower began to fall, and I remember thinking, really, come on. After all, if we are not careful, our minds will always wander to the negative first. Still, then as I attempted to head back to my car to get out of the rain, I looked up and saw a beautiful rainbow, and then I felt God speaking to me as He said, without the rain, you cannot experience the rainbow (or the blessings).

With God, there are no mistakes, my friends, only opportunities. If you have walked away from His will and have dug a hole for yourself, the first step is to stop digging, stop making wrong choices and seek God. He has a wonderful future in store for those who are called according to His purpose, a hopeful future, a future of plenty, and He will work it outright where He has you. After all, without pain, there cannot be the satisfaction and the joy of success. No pain, no gain, they use to say! Joseph must have prayed a lot; I know this well, for in my own life, when traveling through the darkest of valleys, prayer is what keeps me connected to the source of good and righteousness. Prayer is like a bungee cord that pulled me back from darkness into the beautiful, life-giving light of God.

Where do you find yourself spiritually speaking today? Have you caused yourself some troubles as I did? Are you in a place today due in part to the mistreatment of others? Is God once again permitting it all to develop you so that you can get frustrated and fall farther apart from Him, or so that in an act of faith, you may draw ever so closer to Him? Whatever others may have intended in our lives, never forget that God can bring good out of it. God has meant it to produce a blessing in your life and the life of others around you.

So what will you do with that knowledge? I suggest we begin by praying and seeking God's direction. Please, join me in prayer even now. Father in heaven, thank you for Your goodness. Thank you for all that you do for me. Thank you for how you prepare me even in the middle of painful situations, unimaginable separations, and rejection of others. You are indeed working hard at healing my hurt, reconnecting me to loved ones, and transforming me through an intentional time of development. Continue Your work in my life, I pray. As the crucible and fires of Your will continue to melt away the imperfections of my life, as the dross of impurities remains attached to Your final product, please chisel it away.

As we experience distress, pain, discomfort, and hurt, may we know without a doubt that you God always knows best. Let us hope in that fact and know that Your will is good, and even in times of personal reformation, the end product will result from Your good and perfect will. Therefore, just like Joseph, when faced with trials, let us take the higher ground to love and forgive our adversaries rather than retaliate against them. Help us live by Your inspired principles and values, LORD, rather than by the world's standards. May we raise above human standards and not be reactive in dealing with each other.

In my journey, whether it was the breakdown of the relationship with my wife or the total meltdown of my relationship with my ministry supervisors, God, you used that time to help me to find peace in the space between what was and what can be! Instead of trying to prove I was right and keep my focus on the past, God, you granted me opportunities to forgive and forget the past as He often does with us and learn to live in the hope that only He provides. As a result, I was able to leave behind the wrongs and mistakes of the past and begin to rebuild my relationship with my wife and, most importantly, my relationship with you, LORD. Yes, ministry looks different these days than it did once; I'm even practicing my priestly calling under a different banner and even under a different setting, yet God's name is being glorified, and that's what matters. Because You God are a God of mercy and Hope, and it is in that hope that I try to look for in my life these days.

Yes, I still hope for some of those ministry opportunities that I squandered in my poor choices to be returned, and who knows, maybe one day, if it is God's will, it will be so. In the meantime, I am seeking to continue growing with you, God seeking to make amends when possible and focusing ahead on what can be rather than on what was. As we journey through these seasons of brokenness and wilderness, may we never take our eyes off you, the founder and perfecter of our faith. In our suffering, may we see the hope that is found in Christ alone. He who promises to be with us and never to leave us or forsake us. Thank you, Father, for Your love and grace and mercy, indeed transform me, I pray, help me to continue to seek you more intimately through prayer and the study of Your Word. And as I do that to learn to trust that you can use all things for good. You can indeed bring about a blessing to us and others as a direct correlation of our spiritual journey. Thank you for that arduous journey, which we believe will one day lead us into a blessed eternity with you. This, we genuinely believe today and pray for its purpose through the mighty name of Jesus. Amen.

Questions to keep exploring.

Why does God allow such difficulties to come our way? Why doesn't He just sit us down and tells us how it needs to be and demand our obedience?

Why might a lesson be better learned through pain and sorrow?

What conclusion might you be able to deduce from your current situation and how God might already be using it to bless others?

Perhaps you have already experienced a similar painful situation in your walk with God. How has He used it to help others? Have you openly shared it with those He has lead you to?

Do you ever get ahead of God's purpose and get yourself into trouble? How have you been able to slow down and trust in God's sovereignty?

4

———◆•◆•◆———

MOSES

A Wilderness Experience Brought Upon
Another and Another.
A lifetime of struggles that were utilized to free a nation.

"THE LORD's dearest one rests safely on Him. THE LORD
always shields him, and he rests on God's chest.
Deuteronomy 33:12 (CEB)

L iving the good life is something that we may all have
dreamed about at one point or another in our lives. We all
dream of the possibilities when the lottery is at half a billion
dollars!!! (Or maybe it's just me!) Even still, when we are going
through a time of severe need and want, we might find ourselves
wishing for the things others have, their resources, their comforts,
and the apparent worry-free lifestyle that their wealth seems to
bring them. You have heard it said that money doesn't buy you
happiness, but it can sure buy you plenty of things that can make
you happy. Really then the saying should be, money cannot bring
you joy! Unless I suppose you are constantly giving it away to
bless others. After all, happiness can be a fleeting thing, based

on circumstances, but joy can be ever-present in spite of our situation.

We have looked so far at the experiences of Adam and how he was able to find joy in God's redemptive love. We've covered Job and how he found joy in God's faithfulness and restoring grace. Joseph was our third character study so far, and he learned all about joy in God's lifelong preparation and provisions. So now we naturally come to Moses, who will discover the joy that comes from trusting in God's promises, even if it takes a lifetime to manifest themselves. Moses' wilderness experiences, much like in the life of all the Biblical characters we are studying together, are connected to what God wants to do not merely in his life but for the sake of others.

While through Joseph, God intended to save the beginnings of a nation, a mere 70 people. Through Moses's struggles, He plans to save millions and fulfill an ancient promise to make them a nation! And you thought you knew pressure in your life! In his journey through a literal wilderness, Moses will grow from a pampered rich prince to a man who learned to live under the goodness and provision of God, and then finally one of the most outstanding leaders that human history has ever known. I am not simply speaking about the type of leader the world says we should be, but truly a servant leader. A leader who was willing to ultimately trust in God for directions and purpose but also a leader who was capable of standing before God and interceding on behalf of his people. A stubborn, stiff neck, disobeying, untrusting, wishy-washy, backward-looking, did I say stubborn already, an unwilling bunch of people. But don't be so harsh on them; after all, I am sure each of us can relate to one or two of those descriptions in our walk with God.

As unworthy as we may judge them to be from our own lives' perspective, they were and remained till this day, God's chosen nation. A nation chosen to be a beacon of hope, a standard of righteousness for all other nations to follow. To carry His name to the world. To live a different life, set aside, a life based on the hope of a benevolent and merciful God rather than on the whims of man and their false created images. In William Shakespeare's famous Romeo and Juliet play, after the young lovers find out that they each belong to opposing feuding families, Juliet asks a powerful question when she says, "what's a name? A rose by any other name would still smell as sweet." Yet, names are important, and they carry significant meaning. Her point is that maybe their love should not be so disrupted, no matter their family differences. Because their heritage had been one of hatred and discontent, it did not mean that now they could not produce a different fruit of love and care.

The name Moses in Scripture means drawn out (Exodus 2:10 CEB), and if you remember the accounts of his early life, you would see how this fits him perfectly. What's in a name then we would ask? Moses' wilderness experience began even before his life took any shape. As a baby, he was caught up in Pharaoh's fear when he decided to thin out the rapidly multiplying Hebrew population within his nations that had originally made their way down to Egypt, almost four hundred years before through the faithful work of God in the life of Joseph.

Allow me to remind you of Moses' story. His mom wanting to save his life, placed him in a basket and hid him by the river's edge under the watchful eyes of his older sister Miriam. Soon enough, the Pharaoh's daughter came down to the river one day and discovered the baby boy. Recognizing him as a Hebrew child, she sought the assistance of a Hebrew woman, under the suggestion of the guardian sister, to nurture the child and help raise him. Think about God's goodness and His ultimate sovereignty over our lives here for a second and how Moses' life relates to that of his great great great great uncle Joseph. What Pharaoh had intended for evil (destroying all young babies), God will use it for good.

So much so that even after his mother hides him by the water, ultimately God returns him to her now under the protection and provision of Pharaoh's daughter herself to be nurtured. Moses is granted the opportunity to grow up with his own Hebrew culture and traditions, and when he was of sufficient age, he gets to move into the palace and begin his life of luxury! You may say, wait, I thought he was going to live a tough life? See it this way. God will prepare Moses through education and experience that he might not have been able to assimilate any other way. God produced a leader who would stand up to the many challenges yet to come. From the cover of this book, you can see that my name is Moy; it's a simple nickname for my full name, which is Moises, meaning Moses in Spanish. In Latin, Moses is spelled Moyses, which I wish I could say that's where my nickname comes from; that would have been cool, but not. It's just an abbreviation of the Spanish version! While I am no Moses, I have often found comfort in the journey of my namesake when looking at my own wilderness experience.

It is a name that has helped me to find courage in times of waiting, purpose in times of wondering, and faith in times of uncertainty. I haven't always been successful at it, but neither was the original Moy! Soon enough, around the age of 40, the boy Moses is now a grown man who will again need God's help to be drawn out of the troubles he will find himself in. Seeing the suffering of his people under the brutal and bullying rule of the Egyptians, he decides to take matters into his own hands and ends up killing a soldier who was mistreating a Hebrew man. Long story short, Pharaoh seeks to kill Moses for his actions, and Moses finds himself running away for his literal life straight into the desert.

I suppose this too reflects my journey. I, too, saw injustices and attempted to correct them. I picked a fight with a powerful ruler. Perhaps I wounded him, his pride, maybe he felt threaten by an arrogant young servant, and ultimately I too had to run away to an unknown faraway land we call Florida! I may have actually arrived at the promised land; I love Florida!!! We know throughout Scripture that God ultimately brings Moses to a Kenite family under the leadership of Jethro, a priest of Media. While with him, Moses finds a wife and establishes his own family. Additionally, for the next 40 years, unbeknown to him, Moses learns how to survive in desert conditions. How to depend on God's favor and provisions, and how to sustain his life by using God's gifts in nature. Believe me, if you know what happens in the next stage of Moses' life, he will one day be grateful for all of this wilderness training.

What's in a name, we may ask again? Moses' Father-in-law is identified by two heretical names, a Kenite and a Midianite. Midianites are believed to have been descendants of Abrahams from one of the other wives he had, after the birth of his two more famous sons Ishmael and Isaac. Isaac, of course, being the direct descendent of the twelve tribes of which Moses is a part of the Levite clan. Jewish scholars believe that these two terms of Midianites and Kenites refer to the same people. The Kenites being traced by their ancestry back to Cain himself, yes the rebellious son of Adam. Here we see God's prevenient grace at work. He was bringing Moses full circle, even while in the wilderness, connecting him to a people who had already lived in what God Himself described as the Promise Land. A distant family that will one day join and travel with the Hebrew nation once they leave Egypt (1 Samuel 15:6 CEB) and eventually be absorbed into the tribe of Judah itself (1 Samuel 27:10, 30:29 CEB). Which is the lineage of our LORD and Savior Jesus. Fascinating, isn't it? How it is all connected!

Ultimately, after living in the desert for 40 years, Moses' time has finally come, and little does he know that now God will call him to put all of his wilderness and previous princely training into practice at the age of 80! You see, I have learned that God does not waste our times of struggles, but He always uses them to accomplish his purpose. God hears the cries of his people in Egypt and sends Moses to set them free. This would not be the simple task we may have all been led to believe in our young Sunday School Classes. After all, Moses had initially fled Egypt after he killed a man, a fact that I am sure would not simply be overlooked if he entered the City again.

Not only that, he would somehow need to convince a powerful ruler to release an entire enslaved population which was undoubtedly responsible for much of the wealth, prosperity, and prestige which Egypt enjoyed. A truly impossible task, right? Yes, a task that a mere man would not be able to accomplish, but one that would require the ongoing assistance and intervention of God. It reminds me of the Apostle Peter's statement to Jesus later on in the book of Matthews 19:26 (CEB) when he highlights the impossibility of faithfully following Jesus to which Jesus responds, "its impossible for human beings, but all things are possible with God."

Perhaps Moses had a similar question of God, and God's response would have been the same. For you alone, this is impossible, but with my guidance, we will be successful; after all, I AM sending you to do this! Through the faithful work of God and Moses' obedience, God ultimately gets Pharaoh to release his people, and out they go on their way to the Promise Land, a land flowing with milk and honey. Well, not so fast. If you recall Moses's accounts, it was not an easy transition out of Egypt. God used ten plagues to ultimately get Pharaoh to submit to His will. Even after the death of his firstborn son with the tenth plague, Pharaoh eventually pursues the Hebrew people with the full might of his army with the intent of returning them into slavery. But God is not done!

He rescued his people from their condition. Not only did God get the Egyptian people to give gifts to the Hebrew nation as they exited, in short plundering Egypt, but now He will soon destroy Pharaoh's Army. In one of the most famous biblical accounts, the parting of the Red Sea, or most accurately translated the parting of the Reed Sea, as in the plants that grow at the edge of many water sources. And yet, after all that they had witnessed, after all, that they had experience, how do you think the people responded to God? By whining and complaining, by being impatient and stubborn. How dare them, right? Let us remember how many times have we begrudged God when we cannot comprehend his complete plan? How often do we return to our old sin, to our slavery, because we are unwilling to trust in God in the face of seemingly impossible situations?

The truth is that we are not much different than the Hebrew Nation, in our discontent treatment of our good Heavenly Father whom, while may permit difficulty to come our way, ultimately works it all out for good, if we remain faithful to him (Romans 8:28 CEB). Do you remember what happens next in the story? For three weeks, this large nation estimated to have been over two million people when we count women and children walked through the desert right up to the edge of the Promise Land. Then, like many of us, when they permitted doubt to enter their hearts, doubt took the form of fear and mistrust.

In our seasons of uncertainty, we must be careful to guard our hearts against our preconceived notions. No matter what may come our way, how our happiness may be threatened, how our joy may be extinguished, we must live right according to God's promises and never stop believing that He will see us through our circumstances. In his capacity as a military leader, certainly a trait he learned while living in Egypt, Moses decides to scout the Promised Land before simply walking in with two million backseat drivers. For forty days, one spy from each tribe wandered around the land, sampling its foods and taking notes on its inhabitants. When they returned to Moses, their report was not a favorable one. These people are giants, and their cities are heavily fortified; their numbers are more significant than ours; proclaimed the more timid of the spies. But not our rising stars. You see, two of the spies were names you may recognize, Caleb and Joshua!

Joshua, who would ultimately take over the leadership of the people of God, and Caleb, who was perhaps one of Joshua's bravest and most efficient commanders, responsible for the defeat of many of the people living in the Promised Land. The other ten spies bought into their doubts and fear, and when they measured their abilities, they clearly felt short. But Caleb and Joshua did not rely on their abilities; they instead decided to put their faith in the God that had freed them from the mighty power of the oppressing Egyptians. Unfortunately, due to the majority's unfaithfulness, Moses is about to enter not the Promise Land but the third and final stage of his wilderness experience. Disbelief you see always brings real consequences.

You don't believe me? What happens when we think we can do anything without any consequence? We usually get caught and pay a heavy price. What happens when we think we can speed down the highways over and over again, ultimately when we least expect it, one day we get caught and have to pay heavy fines. The penalty for disbelief for the nation of Israel will ultimately be their own death. God's anger burns for these unfaithful people to the point where He wants to destroy them all, yet Moses using yet another trait he surely learned while in Egypt, takes on an ambassadors role and pleads with God for the people.

Another name for a peacemaker, or one who is willing to seek alternative solutions, is a servant leader. Moses' intercession on behalf of the people makes him an excellent precursor to Jesus Himself. Let us look at this comparison briefly from the very beginning.

- Like Jesus, Moses was 'no ordinary child' (v.20). The circumstances surrounding the births of both were appropriately extraordinary, and both of their young lives were initially in danger. (Matthew 2:16–17, Acts 7:19–21 CEB)

- Like Moses, Jesus spent his early life in Egypt. (Matthew 2:13-15 CEB)
- Like Jesus (Luke 2:40 CEB), Moses was noted for his wisdom (Acts 7:22 CEB).
- Like Jesus, Moses had a season of preparation. (As we are studying in this book) We know little about the first thirty years of either of their lives. Both spent this time being prepared for the tasks ahead. (Luke 2:52 CEB)
- Like Jesus (John 2:16 CEB), Moses showed righteous anger at sin (Acts 7:24 CEB). However, unlike Jesus, Moses did commit a crime. But God, in His providence, even used his mistakes for good.
- Like Jesus (John 1:11 CEB), Moses was sent by God to rescue his people but was not recognized as such at the time. (Acts 7:25 CEB).
- Like Jesus (2 Corinthians 5:19 CEB), Moses aimed at reconciliation: Moses tried to reconcile the people back to God (Acts 7:26 CEB).
- Like Jesus (John 5:22 CEB), Moses is described as ruler and judge. (Acts 7:27 CEB).
- Like Jesus (Luke 3:22 CEB), Moses heard THE LORD's voice in the desert (Acts 7:31 CEB).
- Like Jesus (John 1:14; 2:21 CEB), Moses recognized that the Holy place was not in a specific religious location, but it was where ever God is present. (Acts 7:33 CEB).
- Like Jesus (John 8:36 CEB), Moses set the people free from oppression (Acts 7:34 CEB).
- Like Jesus, Moses was misunderstood and rejected by his own people. (7:35, 39 CEB).

Friends here is a simple recipe based on Moses' life which God wishes to bring into the life of every believer. His desire is to prepare us to give us the experience to help us accomplish his tasks and develop a Godly character (thicker spiritual skin, the world may say) to see His will through to the end. In Moses, as it is in our lives, it was a simple matter of time! Forty years growing up with and building a relationship with the would-be Pharaoh, plus learning some organizational skills. Forty years of learning to survive off the wilderness and developing leadership skills. Forty years putting it all into practice, servant skills. How does this translate to your own life and journey? In the end, God calls us to be obedient, whether we need to wait 40 years or four months. Here is God's honest truth, obedience towards God means that we agree with God. If we agree with God, then no weapon fashioned against you will succeed. (Isaiah 54:17 CEB).

Did you cause your spiritual wilderness because of poor choices, choices that ultimately God allowed to come your way, or is your wilderness journey ordained by God so that you may once and for all learn to trust, rely on, and follow His will? Not so with the Hebrews; they eventually cry out when they allow fear to dictate their future blessings and proclaim their preference to go back and live as slaves rather than in freedom. They wanted to return to their lost condition for the sake of a worldly desire as simple as food!!!! Yet Moses does not give up on them; he continues to encourage them and proclaims one of my favorite promises from Scripture. He says, don't worry, "THE LORD will fight for you; you just keep still." Exodus 14:14 (CEB). A promise that later on in the Bible, God reminds us through the Psalmist that we ought to learn to be still and know that God is always in control! (Psalm 46:10 CEB)

Through Moses and the Hebrew nation, God was outlining the type of life He desires His people to live, a life that would differentiate them from the rest of the world, indeed to set them apart as an example of how we should all behave. The Apostle Peter, who had the advantage of living side by side for three years with Jesus Himself, spells out this outline in a precise and straightforward way in his second letter, right at the beginning of the chapter. "God has given us all that we need for godly living.

Through Christ, our savior, we have a precious promise to escape sins craving and put our faith in this. We should then add moral excellence to our faith and, to that, add knowledge, self-control, endurance, affection for others, and love. These things will keep us from becoming inactive and unfruitful in our walk with God.

Never forget that we were cleansed from past sins. Seek then cleansing from current ones. Confirm your call and election as His children by how we live out these principles. So that ultimately we may receive a welcome into the eternity of the kingdom of Jesus Christ, our only LORD and savior. (2 Peter 1:3-10 CEB). Living a life of obedience towards God will help us to identify His presence daily in all aspects of our lives to become more familiar with Him. It's like when you buy a car and all of the sudden you begin to see your model of vehicle everywhere. The truth is that all those other similar cars were always there, but now because you are more familiar with that particular model, you recognize it more. Friends, let us look for God in all circumstances, and we will become more accustomed to identifying His presence in all aspects of our lives. And like Moses, our faith will be strengthened. Moses proclaimed as much in Exodus 15:2 (NIV): THE LORD is my strength and my defense… The Psalmist declares it in Psalm 39:7 (CEB) as well… My hope is set on YOU, God!

One last thing. God evidently permitted Moses' wilderness experience to bless Him and this new, fully grown nation. For forty years, they wandered in a big circle, learning to trust in God's provision. He fed them daily, provided water for them when needed, and even says in the Scriptures that their clothing on their backs and sandals on their feet did not wear off! (Deuteronomy 29:5 CEB) How about that for God's provisions. Moses did his job as the shepherd of his sheep, just like Jesus does for us now, and God took care of the rest! You see, a pastor's job is not to fix things but to be a vessel where God's love may genuinely flow into the lives of others. It is not only love but discipline, correction, inspiration, and encouragement. However, not just pastors, it is indeed the duty of every believer to be a beacon of hope, a source of love, where a lost and depraved world can find its way to the Promise Land of God.

Additionally, let us never stop guarding our hearts; in the end, all of the abilities that God had developed in Moses go to his head, and Moses takes credit for an action that God had provided. Silly Moy! Like many believers, Moses' self-confidence had led him to think he could take care of things from now on, but we must never stop depending on God, not ever. As a result, Moses is not permitted to enter the Promise Land when the time comes. And yet, while some may see this as a complete failure in his leadership, I see it as evidence of God's ongoing grace on his people. What do I mean? Well, God knew that occupying the Promise Land would require a lengthy period of war, something for which now our 120-year-old Moses might not have the necessary strength to endure. So after showing Moses the Promise Land from a distance, God takes him home with him. He draws him out one final time.

The Bible says that God buried his body! (Deuteronomy 34:6 CEB) Truly Moses comes to find rest insight of the physical Promise Land, into the eternal Promise Land in God's presence. And we know, of course, that he made it to heaven; after all, later on, both Moses and Elijah appear to Jesus in the accounts of the Gospel (Matthew 17:1-8 CEB). What a fantastic example of a close relationship with our Father in heaven and the trust that we can have that He will always provide for us until our very end here on earth, straight into His gracious arms in heaven. How, then, are we allowing our own wilderness experience to be a blessing to others while helping us mature in our faith? In what ways can we use our life's experiences to bless and encourage others along their journey? Suppose you could see time as God sees it and see the rest of your life and hope your faithful obedience will ultimately grant you eternity with God. Would that knowledge not cause you to live your life for Jesus more practically and intentionally every day?

Then what are we waiting for? The promises of our personable God are true. The Christian faith is different from other world religions. It is based on a personal witness of the goodness of our God and a willful relationship with a compassionate deity, the one, and only true God. Throughout creation, including those characters we have already covered, Adam, Job, Joseph, and now Moses, we see God's guiding hand. Like the Apostles, faithful saints of the faith, and even you and me to those still to come. So what will you do with what God is doing in you, with how He is developing your own Christian life? It's a great practice to give thanks to God for the places He leads us. Places that offer us hope and healing, even places that seem to tear us down, divide us, and restrict us from accomplishing our full potential. Yet, never forget that God, through his providential care of those who call on His name, is providing for our needs, developing a future of hope and joy for us all, and calling us to join the team that will go out to help save others.

How I would love to meet my namesake hero of the faith, Moses, and pick at his brain and learn from his experiences. That I could ask him, how did he do it, how could he walk in the wilderness for such a long time, and although he stumbled a bit at the end, how did he make it through? From the way he lived his life, I would imagine he would say something along the lines of understanding God's timing is always crucial. Seek clarification of God's purpose through intentional acts of intimacy with the Father above. Be still as God prepares you and others around you for the tasks ahead. He will open the right doors at the right time and will grant you the right words to encourage you to go forth.

Perhaps, we are not quite sure what to do next? Well, we will never go wrong with prayer. So I'd like to invite us all now to pray. Right where you are, seek the will of God, seek His presence while

He may still be found. No time to waste, no additional need for commitment to be made. If you have been listening to God's voice and He has been whispering to you, if He has been making you uneasy about something, then move in faith, as Moses did! Do as others have done before us, come to a point in your life now, and make your commitment to God, that He may complete the work of grace He is currently performing in each of us. No time to waste; join me now, in prayer.

LORD, thank you for the excellent way in which you work Your purposes throughout history and through Your servants like Moses. Today, I trust in Your providence over all the events and circumstances in my life. Faithful Father, this life is full of more trouble and tribulation than I can think of, which tend to dominate and distract my hope in you. When I feel slaved to my anxiety, I get defensive and hostile, especially towards you. Forgive me, LORD, and please grant me a big-picture perspective in what you are doing in my life. Let me rest safely in you and shield me from the attacks of the enemy. Grant that I may turn my eyes to heaven to see you and be confident of Your faithfulness, so that as I stand still, anticipating Your perfect will and Your powerful joy, that I may once again be of service to you in my service of others. You know my life, needs, desires, and transformation process; please helped me take an active part in Your plan for my life from this day forth rather than just being a bystander.

Thank you for Your prophet Moses whom you sent our way to encourage us not to give up in the middle of our wilderness experience but to keep moving. Grant us strength and joy directly from you as we seek to inspire others through our understanding of Your grace. Help us to be better, more productive with Your love. Not just because we want to be better people, but most importantly because we are seeking to grow closer to you, the only true higher power. May we be ever so mindful of Your hand working through every stage and aspect of our lives, and may we be ever so willing to move forward in faith.

From Psalm 121:1-8 (CEB), we pray: "I raise my eyes toward the mountains. Where will my help come from? My help comes from THE LORD, the maker of heaven and earth. Hear his promises as you travel through your own wilderness experience. God won't let your foot slip. Your protector won't fall asleep on the job. No! He never sleeps or rests! THE LORD is your protector; THE LORD is your shade right beside you. The sun won't strike you during the day; neither will the moon at night. THE LORD will protect you from all evil; God will protect your very life. THE LORD will protect you on your journeys—whether going or coming—from now until forever from now." For we pray this in the precious name of Jesus, amen.

Questions to keep exploring.

What excuses are you still making about your behaviors that prevents God from using you to the full extent so that others might be blessed?

We often point up for heaven and down to hell, but what if these real places exist as another dimension, perhaps even overlapping our plane of existence. How should that idea make us feel if God and his angels are that close to us, so near to our situation? (Burning bush)

Moses was present with Elijah later on with Jesus; what does this tell you about God's ongoing plan for humanity?

How should Moses' final slip help us realize how careful we must be in consistently maintaining an attitude of gratitude and reverence towards our Holy God?

5

NAOMI AND RUTH

A Wilderness Experience Brought Upon
by Complete Hopelessness.

"Don't urge me to abandon you, to turn back from
following after you. Wherever you go, I will go; and
wherever you stay, I will stay. Your people will be my
people, and your God will be my God." Ruth 1:16 (CEB)

The notion of loyalty should be integrally added to every
relationship we ever pursue, including a relationship with
God and, of course, a relationship with a spouse. Recently,
after several difficult and work-heavy months, a friend must have
recognized my tired face and the fact that I had lost nearly 25
pounds during that time and asked if I was ok. A loaded question,
to say the least, after all, these sort of questions tend to be
superficial, they tend to be asked in passing, and I am not sure
anyone indeed expects an honest response. After all, it could
take a while to unpack such a query! It all depending on what you
may be going through and how you genuinely feel about it all. My
response, as I hope, honest, when I said, that it had just been a

very long three months, and I was grateful for the opportunities the new year might bring. Her response to me seemed to come out of nowhere, and she asked me, Moy, are you going through a wilderness experience? All I could do was smile and reply, yes.

She then asked me, how long had I been there? It was curious that she had such insight, but I suppose God could have been working through her to get me to start talking about my journey. I had to think for a second on her follow-up question and said, seems like about 9 or 10 years. Now, it hasn't been a complete loss in the wilderness experience, I added, but certainly, a back and forth, learning and re-learning lessons that have undoubtedly brought me to the place I am today. Our past has the incredible ability to add inconceivable weight to our present and put an unforgivable drag in our future, that is, if all we do is focus on that past. Yet, no matter how long I have been in this season of my life, the hope of Christ, the hope of His mercy, the hope of a Godly future meant to bless me and not harm me has not always been of help. Yet the bonds of my relationship with God and others have sustained me along the way, have sure been of benefit to my soul, right through all the darkness and fear.

Meanwhile, through it all, my despair has caused me tremendous darkness of the soul on several occasions, yet with God's help, I have been able to hold on to His love, His goodness, His faithfulness and get back to His light. Sometimes despair happens. It reminds me of a bumper sticker I heard they use to have in the 70s. Sometimes you do step in gum while walking on the sidewalk. Sometimes you get caught in the rain for no good reason. Sometimes you lose someone close or dear to you, or you lose a job, a car, a home, and the why is challenging to understand. Whenever we learn from the experience and come to trust in God regardless of the despair in our lives, we can find comfort in the worse of situations. In the story of Naomi and Ruth, we have an incredible series of events that forced them into a wilderness experience that seems to come straight out of a movie.

Because of needs in their native Israel, Naomi's family had relocated to a neighboring country where eventually not only her husband passed away but so did her two sons. In a culture where women heavily depended on the care and provision of the male members of their family, this was certainly a death sentence for Naomi. Naomi's name is usually translated as pleasantness. Yet, upon her return to Bethlehem from the country of Moab, she proclaimed to those who recognized her still that her name should be changed to Mara, for the almighty God had made her very bitter (Ruth 1:20-21 CEB). If we are not careful, our wilderness experience can produce great bitterness in our souls. Have you ever experienced such complete hopelessness that you just resigned yourself to your self-pity, drowned in your own perception of abandonment, your own understanding of God's heavy hand upon you? I know I've certainly had.

In my wilderness journey, on more than one occasion, I have wondered if my name Moises (Moses), with a meaning of "drawn or saved from the waters," truly described my situation. There were times where it felt like it should be more like saved from drowning in water. Yet through this renewal process that God has seen me fit to endure, my name has again regained a beautiful meaning to me. Even as I have felt like drowning on many occasions, abandoned with no one looking out for me, God has been there, I know, keeping an eye on me and eventually rescuing me from the waters of life. May I encourage you that things will get better, I promise you that, and God promises that. Our past actions may hurt, but there is great hope in the future. In fact, at the end of this story of Naomi and Ruth, we will see Naomi regain her pleasantness as she experiences the renewing and providential power of God. As she begins to experience the mercies of God through the new generation, of her grandson

Obed son of Boaz and Ruth, whom by the way is the grandfather of King David! (Ruth 4:17 CEB). More on David in the next chapter.

In the movie Kungfu Panda 2, as Poe the Panda Dragon Warrior discovers his painful past, he is reminded that even though his story might not have had such a happy beginning, it doesn't make him who he is. It is the rest of his story – whom he chooses to be that matters. This bit of wisdom rings loud in the life of anyone that has ever gone through a difficult time or that may have experienced loss. It is undoubtedly the case in the life of Naomi and Ruth. Our power combo, which we will study here and see how they dealt with their own wilderness walk and shaped their future. As a result of their combined experience, the lives of these two women would be forever connected. Through their faithfulness, loyalty, and perseverance, a crucial and beautiful link on God's eternal chain for redemption was established with Ruth's grandson David.

Here is what I know with complete certainty about the lives of Naomi and Ruth. God's promises are always fulfilled when we allow Him to pour in us His hope, and when in turn, we live our lives in that blessed hope. You'll see what I mean in a moment. Naomi's husband was from the Tribe of Judah; you would recognize that as the lineage of Jesus Himself from the accounts of King David. All we know is that he was a man from Bethlehem (sound familiar too) who lived during the time of the Judges. This is well after the time of Moses and Joshua when the Israelites began to be actively rebellious towards God, the I AM who had saved them from Egypt. Naomi encounters unbelievable hardship, as we pointed out when all the men in her life pass away. She was surely ruined. To add to her stress, she had two daughters-in-law sharing some of this brokenness. Naomi's solution to her troubles is to release the young women and encouraged them to go back to their fathers' house to find a new husband and have a chance at a fulfilling life.

Initially, the young women wanted to go with her, and we see that Naomi is genuinely concerned with their future well-being, so she attempts to dismiss them again. One of the daughters-in-law, Orpah, takes her on her offer and returns home, but to her surprise, young Ruth does not. Ruth clings to her and then proclaims some of the most beautiful words of commitment and loyalty you can ever hear, "where you go, I will go, and where you stay I will stay. Your people will be my people and your God my God." (Ruth 1:16 CEB) Because Naomi and her family had been living in the foreign land of Moab, this meant that Ruth was not descended from the 12 tribes that God had previously established. Yet now, she was willing to follow her mother-in-law back to her ancestral home. The fact remains that the relationship between Israel and Moab had always been a contentious one; we learn about the lineage of the Moabite in Genesis 19:30-38 (CEB), where we discover of their relation to the Israelites.

Moab, you see, was a son of Lot, and if you remember your Bible History, Lot was the nephew of Abraham, whom God called to be the father of His nation. You could say then that Moabites and the Israelites were cousins! Or at the very least shared a great grandfather, in the Father of Abraham. The plot thickens, doesn't it? Yet the history between them had not been as familiar as we may like; they hated each other. When Joshua took over the leadership of the people of God and was leading them into the Promised Land, he sent word to the Kingdoms of Moab and Edom, asking them to allow his people to pass through their territory. By the way, the Edomites were descendants of Esau, as in Esau and Jacob, Jacob who later became Israel, yup they were family too. Yet, they both refused them passage through their lands, which caused hardship between them. Family not getting along, that doesn't happen anymore, does it?

Naomi and Ruth began their journey back to the neighboring land of Israel, with no assurance of provision once they arrived or the protection of anyone. In blind faith, you could say they moved! Two women from opposite families, pledging loyalty to each other. I have often wondered about two people who were so different how they could find the effort and energy to choose to live in harmony, yet why is it so different for so many couples to remain faithful to each other? In this book, you have read how I nearly destroyed my relationship with my wife and how I almost lost it all. Sadly, my selfish acts made my wife feel abandoned and unwanted, and it nearly caused me to lose it all.

When something is broken, it often takes some intentional effort to put it back together again or get it working correctly. When a person's heart is broken, when their will is defeated, when their very soul is downcast due to the trials faced in life, a quick fix is not always available and even more not recommended. For you see, a broken heart must learn to trust once more. A fractured will must practice surrendering again and again. A downcast soul must rediscover the meaning and value of waiting upon THE LORD. Yet much like in the life of Naomi and Ruth, and I will add myself here as well if you have experienced brokenness in your life, I am sure you would understand Naomi's comments to her daughter-in-law and friends when she proclaimed that THE LORD's hand was against her.

When my children were little, they read a book that would say that if it walks like a duck and quacks like a duck, it must be a duck. In times of brokenness, our perception misleads us, so it becomes easier to think that if it looks like God has abandoned us, if we feel that God left us, then surely that means that He has. Yet thank God that He does not hold against us this sort of sin of lack of faith in Him. But, God seeks ways to draw us ever closer to Him to reveal His true purpose for our lives. As we have said before, it is our job in these situations to hold even tighter to our fleeting faith and trust that God knows our pain and that He has a beautiful plan for it.

Naomi could have given up; goodness, Ruth could have gone

back to the safety of her family. What in the world persuaded these women to keep moving forward? What molecule of faith remained in them, which allowed them to hope against all hope? To believe that there could be some opportunity in their future to be rid of their pain? Well, the Sunday School answer is always God or Jesus, right? Yet, in this instance, I think we need to look at the third person in the Trinity: the Holy Spirit of God. Jesus told his followers that He had to go so that God would send a companion and comforter. (John 16:7 CEB) Jesus was human and could only exist like you and me in one place at a time. But the Spirit of God is not bounded by those limitations. He hovers over the surface of the earth and is available to God's children from Australia around the world to Asia and from Alaska to Argentina.

In the Wesleyan theological tradition, there is a term called prevenient grace. It is a beautiful term that refers to the grace that God shows us through His Holy Spirit before we ever come to experience His saving grace. Meaning, we like to say that we came to Jesus at this age or another, or that we found THE LORD in our time of sin. The reality, friends, is that you and I had nothing to do with that initial contact, but it was God Himself through His prevenient grace that prompted us to Him, brought us to a desire to want to know Him, to a place where we could make a decision for Christ and surrender our lives to Him. I believe that this same prevenient grace led Naomi and Ruth to a hope they did not see or even could anticipate. I think that this same prevenient grace brings us back from a broken condition, a place where we may have walked away from our faith and nudged us into the truth that we once believed, that if God is for us, who can be against us.

The Scriptures are filled with men and women who experienced adversity, frustration, pain, disappointment, and loss in their lives. Yet, the overarching story of Scripture is God's redemptive work for His children as He seeks to restore us into His image, back into fellowship with Him. Much like in the case of my season of brokenness, it is nearly impossible to see and believe that there is good in front of you, but perseverance is an important key. Keep moving through the storm, and eventually, you'll come out. Hold on to whatever faith you can find no matter how deep your hopelessness may take you, and God will see you through it. When you come on the other side, your experience will be a great testimony, a great tool to be utilized to encourage others who may experience a similar emotional roller coaster ride. The evangelist Smith Wigglesworth (great name) said, "Great faith is the product of great fights. Great testimony is the outcome of a great test. Great triumph only comes from great trials."

When Ruth and Naomi arrived back home, God quickly provided for them in the person of a kin, a man named Boaz. Boaz was these ladies' apparent last opportunity for provisions and security, and although he did not have to, by God's grace, he manages to secure the responsibility for their well-being and cares for them. Eventually, he also accepts Ruth as his wife. Soon after, they have a son named Obed, father of Jesse, father of the anointed boy-king David. You see, I have come to fully understand that when we are going through a wilderness experience and others attempt to encourage us, that often our pessimism in those dark hours can be overpowering. It isn't easy to accept that glimmer of hope that others try to offer us. Yet hope has the possibility of turning into faith, and faith is the reality of what we hope for, the proof of what we don't see. (Hebrew 11:1 CEB) We never despair that we will not have oxygen to breathe, it's always there, and in faith, we take tens of thousands of breaths each day. We must never then dwell in our disappointment, in our sadness, in our despair so much that we become disconnected from reality and never take hold of hope, which, as we said, can grow into persevering faith. Dear reader, God has not abandoned us. He has not left us, just like He never left these two women. Eventually, as God provides for them, Naomi, who had become understandably quite bitter, glorifies God for His provision, especially that of a grandson.

There is a movie I once saw where the main character was playing a scientist, and he explains that the purpose of each cell in our bodies is to pass knowledge along to the next cell and so forth. Now, I don't know if that's just Hollywood movie talk, but it makes sense. We all long to pass our knowledge and experiences to others, and so God has provided a way for us to do it through our children. Immortality is genuinely at our grasp if we teach our children the things we have learned and allow them to advance that knowledge to the next level. Naomi had seen no such possibility. Her husband and sons were dead, and she was in no physical shape to start having children again. Her despair must have accompanied a sadness of not being survived by anyone. When she died, she would be done. Yet God, through Ruth, restored her joy.

Look around you, in the middle of your situation; who is God using to bless you? Who is He using to remind you that He is still very much walking by your side? And all that He requires from you is to stop, be still, and acknowledge that He is God? Can you believe that? I want to encourage you to do what you can, my friend, to believe that God still has a better plan for you than you could ever dream for yourself. That being with Him in His love and His service is still the most important thing that any of us can ever hope to do. Just be still and learn to trust Him again. Be still and seek Him with all of your heart, try and try and God promises that He will be found! (Jeremiah 29:11-13 CEB)

When you feel alone, in the middle of nowhere, don't allow your thoughts or the enemy to lie to you and tell you, you must see this through or pick yourself by your bootstraps. You see, this is very much my character; get up and work harder, stand up and do something else on your feet, soldier, get moving. Yet God wants us to rely on His strength and not our own. Yes, move as you can and move ahead in faith, but when you can't anymore, always rely on God and seek His support. You are not alone. Jesus is alive today and living His life through you if you let Him!

Remember what the Apostle Paul said, "I have been crucified with Christ, and I no longer live, but Christ lives in me" (Gal. 2:20 CEB). Again, Paul says the whole mystery of the Gospel comes down to this: "Christ living in you, the hope of glory" (Col. 1:27 CEB). No wonder God says to us, be still and know that I am God (Psalm 46:10 NIV).

Be still in your loss, be still in your separation, be still in your sadness and discouragement. Be still. Be still. Be still! As you wait patiently on THE LORD, the great I AM's mercy and grace will shine through you, and not only will you experience it, but even more, like in the lives of Naomi and Ruth, many others as well will rejoice that God is truly faithful and good. For He is indeed faithful, and He always provides for His children according to His marvelous riches in glory. Yes, keep moving forward, but do so with purpose, simply knowing that God is on your side, and as we learn to be still, it is then that we will hear the whisper of His Holy Spirit comforting us and bringing us peace in our time of need. That surely was my case.

Are you experiencing failure in a relationship? Then make a conscious effort to recommit to it, to give yourself entirely at reviving said relationship at reestablishing its pillars of loyalty and hope. Leaving all other things behind, submit in total surrender to your spouse, your parent, your children, your friend, whoever it may be, and do not give up on that relationship. Once you commit to this effort in your mind and heart, then comes the hard part, stop, and begin to wait on THE LORD and trust in God to work out the rest.

How do we actually become still? If you are anything like me, this will be a difficult concept to practice. According to my phone app, mostly due to my work environment, I discovered that during the years 2019 and 2020, I walked over 4.3 million steps each year, which came out to a little over 2,300 miles per year. I am constantly moving at work, can't sit still, I suffer, you see, from ants in the pants syndrome! I now know why my knees hurt so much, why I keep needing new shoes. Being still in our trials is a spiritual discipline you see that we must all learn to practice. It doesn't matter how fast or often we move around in our day; we must learn to slow down when it comes to the development of our faith and how we seek God daily. We must be mindful of those things that stress us out, cause us anxiety, recognize them, and find ways to resist them, not to give those situations too much thought. In the end, God is with us, and He will see us through it, even when we cannot know the future. In unexpected situations too, yes mourn, yes feel, but ultimately come back to the source of hope.

Lessons learned during a wilderness experience are not always immediately apparent, but God provides wisdom and understanding with time. I can testify to you that while I still have a lot of learning to do on being still before God, as I look back through my journey so far. I can see the benefits of seeking God first rather than automatically trying to fix things on my own. I can see the practicality of trusting that God is in control of my past, present, and future, rather than running well ahead of Him trying to put the pieces back together. When we stop and let God, we are trusting God, trusting that His promises are true, trusting that He will do what He said He would do because He is faithful! Perhaps Naomi hung on to this bit of hope as she traveled back home.

Sometimes, I like to think if we could sit down with these seemingly simple yet powerful women in the history of our faith and ask them to share some advice. Some pointers on how to deal with our joint endeavors with others. They might say something like: Collaboration is vital and do not perceive others as competitors but as partners. Be supportive and encourage each other, lifting each other as you go along. Have the mindset of others first, look to understand, utilize and maximize the strengths of others. Be sure to set measurable goals to see that together more can be accomplished, that two is always stronger than one!

Remember when we are going through a desperate night of the soul, or a time of wilderness experience, maybe just an outright season of spiritual dryness, and we stop and seek God, what we are saying is, I cannot do it, LORD, I need you. Then and only then can He begin to fill our emptiness, massage our pain away, and provide His peace in our hearts. He does all this by sparking hope once again in us and, as I already mentioned, that hope will grow into faith and that faith, if it's just the size of a mustard seed, can move mountains. Maybe you have suffered similarly lost as Naomi did. Perhaps you encountered uncertainty like Ruth experience. Yet, in the end, let us learn from both of their wilderness experiences, and that is that God remained faithful to them, in the same way that He will remain faithful to you and me.

No matter how hopeless our situation may be, the hope of our salvation is in Christ. The hope of eternal life is in God; the hope that He is drawing us back to Him every day is in His Holy Spirit, so what do we have to lose? You've tried everything else already, right? Why not give God another chance, seek Him, begin to trust Him again, and as He is doing in me, I promise you, He will bring you through and develop in you a stronger, more committed, and faithful heart to carry on the journey of a child of God and a follower of Jesus.

A prayer from Psalm 23

Jesus, You are everything to me. Because you watch over me, LORD, you make sure I am always provided for! You handle my physical needs and my spiritual development. You guide my steps through Your Word right to the place you have set out for me. I experience Your protection around me; it brings me comfort when I find myself in the darkest of valleys. You know me by name; no one can undo Your plans for me. From you, I receive all that

I could ever need, and more! Help me never to neglect Your faithfulness, Your good provisions, Your amazing love, that I may dwell in Your presence forever.

Questions to keep exploring.

If God can use a widow and a foreigner to carry on His eternal purpose, how do you think He can use your willingness trek to serve Him? Ask Him!!!

How can the choices we have made and are currently making influence our lives in the near future? Will that choice point us to the will of God or away from it?

How can you motivate others with the accounts of Ruth and Naomi, who may be going through a strange, complex situation, to stay the course and push ahead?

What stands out to you about Ruth's commitment to follow her mother-in-law where ever she may go, to surrender to her God, and to become part of her people?

What life-changing, world-impacting commitment are you willing to make to God? Do you know what complete surrender would look like in your daily walk with Him?

What is your understanding of the faithfulness of God in your life?

6

—◆◆◆—

DAVID

Multiple Wilderness Experiences
Which All Produced Humility.

"THE LORD is my shepherd. I lack nothing. Even when
I walk through the darkest valley, I fear no danger
because you are with me." Psalm 23:1, 4 (CEB)

We all have bullies in our lives. I certainly do. People who cause us harm for no other apparent reason than their personal satisfaction derived from their ill-treatment of others. Individuals who seem to go out of their way to undo any of our accomplishments and criticize any of our efforts. They thrive on attacking us whether we are at our best or in our lowest conditions. The young man David started his adult life with such a bully. Later on, when he was King, he became his own bully through his careless actions. And finally, towards the end of his life, his son, attempting to overthrow him as King, became that abuser in his life. Thankfully, David teaches us on whom we must focus when we face our bullies, and I'll give you a hint, it's not in ourselves!

If you and I make the mistake of paying too much attention to the bullies in our lives, we run the risk of never fully developing to our full potential. If the opinion of others becomes of greater value to us than what our Creator thinks of us, then surely we are on a path to depression, darkness of the souls, a straight out self-imposed wilderness experience. At the end of the day, no matter what life may bring our way or even what God may permit us to endure, we must be people who long after the advice and direction of God and resist the naysayers. It is how our Creator designed us to live!

One of my favorite authors, Max Lucado, crafted a beautiful and inspiring story in his book "You Are Special" that I would humbly like to share with you. The implications of this story are far-reaching from merely being a children's book, touching even the wisest of adults if we but allow its truths to resonate in our lives. Mr. Lucado introduces us to the Wemmicks, a community of wooden people, and one of their main characters is Punchinello. You see, the Wemmicks would go around either giving each other compliments or criticizing one another. If another Wemmick shared a compliment, they would add a shinny star sticker to their bodies. If criticism were handed down, then a dull gray dot would be attached. It got to be so bad that some Wemmicks were being criticized just because they had too many dots and so more and more dots kept being added on. For those they felt could not do much of anything, a dot was added. If they felt unworthy or sad, a dot was added. If they could not perform a simple task, you guessed it, a dot would be added. Such was the case with Punchinello.

Punchinello would not even go outside anymore. In fear that he would get more dots. And when he ventured outside his door, he would hang out with other gray dotted Wemmicks, to blend in if you will. That is until the day that he met Lucia. You see, Lucia had no shinny stars and no dull gray spots. It's not that people didn't give them to her, Lucado explains; it's just that they did not stick to her! Punchinello thought to himself that this is how he wanted to be, so he asked Lucia how she had accomplished it. Lucia told him a tale of the woodcarver name Eli, whom she would visit daily. After spending time with him, she proclaimed, anything anyone else would say simply didn't affect her. As you can imagine, Punchinello set off to meet this Eli and see what the big deal was all about.

Upon arriving at the woodcarver's home, he had some second thoughts and attempted to turn back, but he heard a voice call his name before he could. It was Eli! Punchinello asked the woodcarver! Sir, you know my name? And Eli replied, of course, I do, I made you. It's so good to see you! Punchinello asked the woodcarver why Lucia had no stars or spots, and Eli told him that it was because the things he said to Lucia were more important to her than the things others thought about her. Then Eli said, Punchinello, the stickers will only stick if they matter to you. Keep coming to see me every day, and before long, all of your spots will fall away, and you will care only what I say to you because I love you, you are special to me, and I don't make mistakes. The moral of the story is simple, and it fits great with our character's humble beginning for this chapter. While man may look at the outside, God knows what we are made of on the inside because He made us, and He makes no mistakes. (1 Samuel 16:7 CEB)

Isn't it a fantastic simple lesson? I thank God for granting Max Lucado the wonderful inspiration to put it into words. This modern-day parable reminds us that it should be what God thinks of us that matters, not others? Yet, I know from personal experience that we are not always good at accepting this simple truth. No, in fact, we tend to rely on the words of others to prop us up, and for some, those words do not serve to encourage us but to reduce us, to make us feel less than worthy, what a bully does. We blindly seek the approval of others, and when all we get is trash back from them, we still accept it, and what's worse, we begin to believe it. When we listen to the wrong voice, it has the effect of tearing us down rather than building us up.

I will never hide the fact that no other person caused many aspects of my own wilderness experience than me. This, of course, does not negate the fact that I still sought the approval of unworthy people, who did not help me but were only interested in defeating and molding me to their antiquated perspectives without appreciating my forward vision and efforts. People who called themselves my friends yet quickly dismissed me and abandoned me when I needed them the most. When I had more spots than stars, they added more spots, and even as I ran from them, the spots kept getting added. Yet, I admit again, I am to blame for much of it. I do not say this to brag but to confess my own inabilities and shortcomings. It was my selfishness, my rebellion, my constant poor choices that led me down a path of discontent, anger, of grief, a path where I had fought hard to gain the approval of others, but it was to no avail. For even as they gave it, it was soon taken away when I tripped and fell in my spiritual walk. Oh, how I wish they had caught me when I fell, rather than trample me. But that was then, and God certainly dealt with me differently. He did not focus on my shortcomings but the content of my character, the makings of my heart. These days, I need to focus on my relationship with God so that not even I can add dots to myself when I am feeling especially low.

You see, I have often thought of a wilderness experience as an interruption, a necessary one at that, so it seems! I thought I had it all figured out; all of my ducks appeared to be in order. Family, ministry, education, and youth!!! I focused so much on what I had achieved that I neglected the single most influential force that got me to where I was, and that was my relationship with God. Maybe things were going well for you, but now it's time to pause and test your faith in some way, so here comes the wilderness. This has also been the case for all the characters we have studied so far, including many more to come. Certainly, this was the case of young David. A shepherd by trait, a lonely job to say the least, but a time when he perfected his musical ability and honed his slingshot skills. For David, this was a time when he undoubtedly learned to seek God and spend time with Him; after all, there is not much else to do when watching over sheep.

This was David's first actual wilderness, and he was surrounded by sheep who do not care for even what is best for them or how wild animals stand ready to scoop them up as a free meal. I wonder what emotional stages David traveled between during this time. As he practiced his music or his rock-throwing, as he led his flock to greener pastures, how did his emotional state hold up? I don't know if you can relate, yet in the middle of my own wilderness experience, even as family and activities surrounded me, I have felt the cold touch of loneliness. I have felt very much interrupted from my previous busy life into this time of seemingly unending waiting. Interruptions that I can give thanks to God now, that I am on the other side of those depressing seasons, thankfully because I can look back and see what He was doing all along. I'm sure David often looked back at the blessing of those quiet days when he had to deal with being a King and even later on with his overly deceptive son.

Before long, David's perceived simple lifestyle is interrupted when God decides that he will be the next King of Israel. At least David must have thought, after I am sure feeling insecure and unworthy of such an appointment, finally, I will get to do some good, I will get to affect change to help people in need and bring glory to God. That's what I use to think. I felt untouchable; after all, I was doing the work of God. I was a self-appointed defender of all things Righteous, all things God; what a fool I was, I am truly sorry to all those that had to deal with my arrogance in those days. I hope you can forgive me.

Yet, as we see in David's story, that would not be the case, not for some time. Why? Because crazy, madman King Saul is still on the throne. Wait, so God anointed two kings? Yes, David was to be Saul's replacement! And what's worse, Saul knew it! "Replacement" a word that any sitting monarch or president or ruler loves to hear, right? Hi, my name is David, and you are sitting in my chair!!! From the moment that David demonstrated his incredible aptitude to trust in God and faced a literal gigantic bully whom he defeated in the name of THE LORD, David's life became one interruption after the others. One word of praise from some and an expression of criticism from others. Some were, of course, out of his control, perpetuated by the jealous King, and others were self-inflicted wounds that would cause him great additional pain and frustration later on in his life.

Yet God is always faithful, and thanks to the Psalms, we can get a front seat to the emotional rollercoaster that will be David's life. A detailed description of the frustrations he caused himself or the hurts others attempted to bring upon him. We always experience the same result where we see a good God who reshapes those situations into His will. From joy to depression, from whining to expectation, from fear to courage, and so much more. On several occasions, in fact, David finds himself reliving a wilderness experience. Yes, first as a young child, alone tending sheep. If you are an introvert, perhaps this can be an enjoyable time, yet the sheer seclusion can drive one mad if you are not. Next, as we already alluded, he is being chased by the mad King threatened by the young man, so much so that he is bent on killing him. Yes, you heard that right. God anointed David as the next King, but the current King is not going to go down without a fight, a selfish attitude that will ultimately cost Saul not just the kingdom but his life as well. Later on in his life, David commits adultery, murder and completes the sinner's trifecta by lying about the whole thing and covering it up. But he is not done; even later on in his later years, David is called to suffer through his own son, Absolom's actions, who attempt to steal his father's throne.

We must be able to examine our lives and our actions each

day to help us identify when we may be flirting with sin, when we may be standing at the edge of a sinful decision. That is to say, when one simple step, or decision, or word will cause us to sin. As we do, let us ask, are we taking our commitment to God and the expectations He places on our service seriously? Are we deliberately seeking God? Are we daily developing our faith in God? Beware of contentment, not where you find peace in all situations but in the negative sense where you begin to think you are done and that there is nothing else for you to do or learn. God is never done with us.

David experienced such a negative side of contentment, which led him to agony and suffering. According to the Scriptures, when Kings were supposed to lead their armies, David is at home being lazy, sleeping to all hours of the day. I'm sure it was a beautiful spring day, and we all know how hard it is to get out of bed on days like those! This out-of-character behavior causes David to be in the wrong place, at the wrong time where he identifies Bathsheba from the roof of his house. A decision, a word, a selfish action that would bring great distress and sorrow to his life. Can you relate? I think I can if I think it through. As I've mentioned, I have felt alone before; I have felt the attacks of others in my life, motivated perhaps by their jealousy and insecurity. Yet, I have also brought pain on myself by lying, manipulating; I have even lost all that I counted dear because of my own selfish decisions. I had become complacent and thought there was nothing else God could teach me.

Oh yes, David and I drank from the same fountain of dissolution and loss, the ever-flowing waters of self-pride and self-righteousness that usually leads to a wilderness of hopelessness. You see, when we attempt to cut corners in our life choices, whether it is to hide sin or to achieve a result faster than intended, we will always be left with an incomplete picture. When we allow situations or others to instigate us or rush us in our decision-making, it will always lead us to poor choices. And poor choices

David did make! Let us learn to follow the standards of God rather than our mere desires. Surrendering to our impulses will often cause us to get ahead of God's plan. Stop. Slow down. Be still before God! Seek to be held accountable by God as you follow through and persevere on His promises and discipline for your life. There was a Sunday School song I use to sing in Spanish that would say, "be careful my little eyes what you see, be careful my little hands what you touch, for THE LORD is up above and He sees my every act." We sure learned many things as youngsters that still should apply to our daily life, didn't we? David should have remembered the songs he learned as a child!

Yet, if you have ever read through the Psalms or the books of Samuel, you will discover one thing without a doubt, and that is that David was a man that knew where to find hope. Despite the real-life situations, he knew where to go to bathe in the hope of God. I can also testify that this is part of the work of grace that I feel God has been doing in my own life during my wilderness journey. That no matter what I may be going through, my hope must be built on nothing less than the mercies of God, for He is at work in my life in every situation, truly working it all out for good, according to His purpose, not mine. So I remind us, be careful little eyes what you see!

David says as much in Psalm 56, "When I am afraid, I will trust in you. In God, whose Word I praise, In God I trust; I will not be afraid. What can mortal man do to me?" (Psalm 56:3-4 CEB). Or who can forget good old faithful Psalm 23, "Even when I walk through the darkest valley, I fear no danger because you are with me? Your rod and your staff—they protect me, Yes, goodness and faithful love will pursue me all the days of my life, and I will live in THE LORD's house as long as I live." (Psalms 23:4, 6 CEB). We find a similar tone, yet with a more profound promise in Psalm 138 where David proclaims: "Though I walk in trouble, you preserve my life. You stretch out your hand against the anger of my foes; with your right hand, you save me. THE LORD will vindicate me;

your love, LORD, endures forever—do not abandon the works of your hands." (Psalm 138:7-8 NIV).

Our own weaknesses, friends, can sometimes lead us to desire and want things that are not the things God wants and desires for us. Weakness towards the opposite sex can also equal real danger. Weakness towards addictive substances can cause us much pain. Weakness towards the evil of the world, such as corruptive power, the love of money, and possessions, can lead us down a terrible path. Weakness is expressed when we allow fear to rule our lives rather than trusting in God in all circumstances. Flaws that lead us to sinful opportunities, and like spiritual fools, we give into them. Having a good friend, someone who can keep our focus will be beneficial in these times of poor decision making.

David had such a friend in Jonathan who was looking out for him, even though he was the Mad King's son. In my own experience, I lost all my so-called friends; for some reason, I was cut out from everyone: it was indeed a triple breakup. With my wife with my lifelong ministry, and with my friends. My heart hurt so much as I focused on the why rather than looking at what God was working out through me. During my dark times, a very good friend, one of the two or three that have remained in contact with me, said Moy, we need to pray for a miracle! And I remember his prayer. Recently I connected with that good friend, and as I shared the good news of God's ongoing restoration in my life, he recalled how we had prayed for a miracle, and we were able to glorify God. Thank you, Jordan! Someone once said that a miracle seems impossible, but it happens anyway. That's what God will do in your life as we learn to draw nearer to him every day rather than focus on our troubles or what others may think of us.

Much like the Wemmicks of Max Lucado's story, David was often too focused on the thoughts of others. I mean, he knew the master, his Creator. Yet, he often became very inward focus. Let me tell you from personal experience that if you only look inward and not around you, you will eventually run into something, as you cannot tell where you are going. I am not talking about a wall or an actual hole in the ground, but I am talking about a spiritual wilderness experience. We have previously discussed the case of Joseph and how God can and does use our wilderness experience to develop a stronger character. A more determined will for His purpose for us, so even as you feel interrupted in your life because you must now endure this time of difficulty, remember, God is with you.

In David's own words, God's staff, which is meant to guide us and protect us, is with us, and yes, his rod, which is a disciplinary tool used to correct the wayward sheep, will also accompany us. (Psalm 23 CEB) There have been many lessons learned during my own wilderness experience, and one of them is that character development, or spiritual growth, goes hand in hand with discipline. And by that, I don't mean a daily beating, but the gentle realignment of a master who wants us to focus on him, a maker who wants us to only care about what He has to say. After all, remember Scripture also reminds us that THE LORD disciplines whomever He loves. (Hebrews 12:6 CEB). Think of your car when it is out of alignment; it pulls to one side or the other. When our spiritual alignment is not tuned up with God, we get pulled from one side to the others until it gets corrected. Much like with our vehicles, an alignment takes a small bit of weight, just enough pressure to get us on the straight n narrow again.

What stage of your wilderness experience are you currently traveling through today? A simple word of advice, do not fret, but know that God loves you, that He cares for you, and to quote Max Lucado again, "He loves you just the way you are, but He doesn't want you to stay that way, but He wants you to be more like Jesus." David often cries out in the Psalms when he feels God a bit distant, yet God never left him. It reminds me of that poem, the footprint on the sand. When we feel alone, God is still with us. When we feel persecuted, pressed on all sides, God is with us, especially when we feel defeated by our bullies. God is with us. David, yet again out of the fount of his own experience, encourages each of us from Psalm 37:1-9 (AMP), where we read:

- "Do not worry because of evildoers, nor be envious toward wrongdoers; For they will wither quickly like the grass, and fade like the green herb."
- "Trust with full confidence in THE LORD and do good; Dwoll in the land and feed on His faithfulness.
- Delight yourself in THE LORD, And He will give you the desires and petitions of your heart.
- Commit your way to THE LORD; trust in Him also, and He will do it. He will make your righteousness like the light, And your judgment like the noonday sun.
- Be still before THE LORD; wait patiently for Him and entrust yourself to Him; Do not whine or agonize because of him who prospers in his way, Because of the man who carries out wicked schemes.
- Cease from anger and abandon wrath; Do not fret; it leads only to evil. For those who do evil will be cut off, But those who wait for THE LORD, they will inherit the land."

It isn't easy to find hope in the present moment of a wilderness experience, and it seems too distant and out of reach. Still look back, even now, into your life and ask God to show you how He has always been with you, guiding you and strengthening you even when you were at your lowest and ultimately thank Him as you begin to recognize His hand of restorations and purpose in your life. Many were the nights that I wasted in tears, in self-pity, drowning in my own perceived hopelessness, only to discover years later the closeness of my father in heaven who saw me through it all with the help of the last few friends I had and one new one in particular. I have shared how many things God has already restored to me, many things that I have desired for, He has undoubtedly bestowed upon my life, others I still pray one day will be made available again if they are what is good for me.

Your wilderness experience will not last forever, even if you perceive it to be so in your mind. No, God has a purpose, even if it means you must get chased by a madman across the land. God's will cannot be stopped by the doing of another person, even your poor choices will only delay it for a time, but God remains faithful to us, no matter what, especially when we repent of our selfish actions and return to His perfect will. Even though he walked through the valley of shadow and death several times, David still experienced great blessings from God. Even though a crazy King wanted him dead, David eventually assumes the throne. Although a great sin caused him the life of his child, through the next child with Bathsheba, Solomon fulfills even more of God's promises for His people. And while one of his kids, Absalom, attempted to take it all from him, ultimately God used others to put this insurrection down and maintain His promises to David.

Yes, it is clear that a wilderness experience is meant to humble us, take away our pride, clear out any self-righteousness, empty our cups to such a state that we then become ready to be filled by God. Focus only on our maker and seek His strength, courage, and will to keep going. That is from the one trustworthy source of love and life and not from a passing thing, such as an external relationship, a frustrating job, or the latest self-help book. (Of which this is not one of them!) David's recipe out of the wilderness is also a recipe for success in life. Don't worry but trust in God. Delight in Him, and He will answer your prayers according to His will. Surrender to Him even in your worst spiritual battles, be still before your God, and wait for His goodness to shine through. (Psalm 37 CEB) He promised to do as much, and after all, God is faithful, and He will do what He said he would do.

Because of David and God's intimate connection and faithful service, God made an everlasting promise to keep a member of his family on the throne always. David, who hailed from the tribe of Judah, would be responsible for the lineage that brought us, Jesus, not just through Joseph but also through Mary. You see, if you follow the genealogy presented in the Gospel according to Matthew, we find the line trace backward from Joseph through Solomon back to David. Additionally, in the Genealogy presented in the Gospel according to Luke, we see the same divine line traced back from Mary through another one of David's sons, Nathan. From genealogical accounts, David traces this ancestry even further back to Abraham and even Adam, making David truly a central player in the perpetual redemptive work of God.

As a result, it is easy to see David as a precursor of Jesus the Christ and also as a proper representative of the first human, Adam. As a result, when you read about David, hopefully, you can find an excellent connection between the two. As a man, he sure sinned, as Adam did, yet as a divinely appointed ruler, he watched over the people and provided for their needs. As a man, he made irrational decisions that often got him in some sort of trouble. Yet as a duly appointed servant of God, he brought about the righteousness of God and set the stage for our savior Jesus. It is in these similarities that I find comfort; in fact, at the end of his ministry here on earth, Jesus gives His followers the great command to go and make disciples (Matthews 28:19-20 CEB). This would set the stage for the future of the Christian church, God's surprise to the world, the hands and feet of God here on earth.

We can look at David and his leadership styles and see a similar pattern. Although he failed from time to time, he understood the need to "Go" to train, share authority, trust, and follow up with his followers. Even as he fell short of God's glory, he understood the need to get into action, setting others lose to multiply his example and successes, granting them responsibilities, empowering them, and revisiting and adjusting the goals as necessary. Lastly, even as David tripped over his own pride and indifference, he still fully grasped the meaning of the word "All," he knew God had him where He needed him for the people's sake, that they might hold him accountable too as their leader for the powers he possessed so that he might become a true servant and lead God's nation to succeed in upholding the requirements of a Godly relationship. You and I are like David, shoot, we are like Adam, yet God calls us to be like Jesus, to intentionally leave our sin behind and trust in God's leading, to faithfully, go and make disciples of all nations for the glory of God.

Your wilderness experiences are a time for training and development, now get up and get to work under the complete guidance of the Holy Spirit, in the name of Jesus and for the glory of God. Just a few final words of encouragement from David himself found in Psalm 30 (CEB), as he is detailing God's deliverance from his many wilderness experiences:

"I exalt you, LORD, because you pulled me up;
you didn't let my enemies celebrate over me.
LORD, my God, I cried out to you for help,
and you healed me.
LORD, you brought me up from the grave,
brought me back to life from among those going down
to the pit. You who are faithful to THE LORD,
sing praises to Him; give thanks to His Holy name!
His anger lasts for only a second,
but his favor lasts a lifetime.
Weeping may stay all night, but by morning, joy!

When I was comfortable, I said, "I will never stumble."
Because it pleased you, LORD, you made me a strong
mountain. But then you hid your presence. I was terrified.
I cried out to you, LORD. I begged my Lord for mercy:

"What is to be gained by my spilled blood,
by my going down into the pit?
Does dust thank you?

Does it proclaim your faithfulness?
LORD, listen and have mercy on me!
LORD, be my helper!"
You changed my mourning into dancing.
You took off my funeral clothes and dressed me up in joy
so that my whole being might sing praises
to you and never stop.
LORD, my God, I will give thanks to you forever."

Questions to keep exploring.

How are you seeking God's will during your times of spiritual darkness? (Matthew 6:33 CEB)

How are you relying on THE LORD's care over every aspect of your life during your trials? (Psalm 62:8 CEB)

Are you living by what you know rather than what you think? Trusting in your faith in God. (Mark 11:22-24 CEB)

Have you ever wondered if God was simply done with you and had decided to move on to someone else? Have you ever thought that you can still be of service to Him?

Who is that friend that has stood by you through thick and thin? Have you expressed your appreciation to them? Have you witnessed how their support has helped you carry on in full confidence of God's goodness for you?

7

———◆•◆•◆———

ELIJAH

A Wilderness Experienced Initiated by Fear and Doubt.

"Elijah was terrified. He got up and ran for his life. He went
farther on into the desert a day's journey. He longed for
his death: "It's more than enough, LORD! Take my life..."
1 Kings 19:3-4 (CEB)

've heard it said that if you are out leading a group of people
and turn around and no one is following, that you are merely
going out for a walk. For so long in my journey, I have been
granted the title of leader or officer or shepherd, most recently
pastor, and yet only to discover that no one is following, I'm just
waking around aimlessly; at least it feels that way. Then I realize
that even those who go from place to place bringing the message
of God's hope are not aimless wanderers, but they are honest
servants of God—accomplishing His will. Kind of like the old-time
traveling evangelist! I think from now on, perhaps I would prefer
the designation of servant evangelist, especially in the ministries
that God seems to keep me floating to and from. Many of the Old

Testament prophets lived a similar life, as it turns out. This is no more evident than with God's evangelist servant Elijah!

Elijah was a Prophet who ministered doing the time of King Ahab. He has the privilege to be the seventh king over the people of the Northern Kingdom Israel, yet also carried the unfortunate title of the King who did the most evil in the sight of God. Scripture spells it out when it says, "Ahab did more to anger THE LORD than all Kings of Israel before him" (1 King 16:33 CEB). That's a heck of a statement. Other translations use the word provoke, which is usually a negative-sounding word, yet this man was fearless; you could say, maybe he did not care or didn't see his actions as evil. Yet, he was so evil, "how evil was he?" He was so evil that he married an evil woman on top of all he did to anger God. Jezebel was her name. She was a foreigner to the laws and requirements of God for His people; therefore, soon enough, she had her husband worship the wrong God, Baal. (1 King).

She was so evil that one of her first actions after becoming queen was to get rid of many of God's Prophets by murdering them. A contemporary prophet of Elijah was Obadiah, and he took it upon himself to hide and save many of these servants of God who were running for their lives (1 King 18:13-14 CEB). And still, her evil deeds continued. These were horrible people; we could say they were truly satan's power couple, and they were in charge! It reminds me of some of the really bad leaders we have had in our most recent history. Yet these folks will do some terrible things before they are done. Then enters our Prophet Elijah, who gives a simple message to the King concerning an upcoming drought. Elijah makes it clear that it is not he who is causing him trouble, but the King himself because of his evil actions has brought this judgment on the people. Everything that ensues is an epic battle between good and evil, where THE LORD's goodness eventually triumphs.

We jump then right into the Prophet's life, where Elijah is

coming off an incredible high. We have been there, experience a mountain top transformation at a Christian retreat or other church activity that filled us with the desire to go back down into the valley and save the world for Jesus! When I was fourteen, and I made a conscious decision to follow Christ through the nudging of the Holy Spirit, my heart was filled with passion and excitement. I was ready to go and tell others about Jesus. Because I was born in a Christian home, I often thought that because my parents were Christian pastors that this must of meant I was a Christian too. I know, I should have paid closer attention in Sunday School. Nonetheless, I was ready to take on the world with my newfound spiritual fervor. Unfortunately, I allowed poor choices to drown that first love excitement.

Perhaps you can relate to my experience and join me in testifying that it doesn't always translate into effective Christian service just because we have a mountain top spiritual experience. During my pastoral years, there were other times when coming off this experience meant I would try to institute new ministries, new outreach efforts, only to encounter opposition and denominational restriction. It was like a bucket of cold water being poured on my newly reignited zeal! On one of my last experiences after completing a wonderful leadership training program in Canada, called Arrow Leadership, under the guidance of Dr. Steve Brown, I felt the transforming hand of THE LORD upon my life. It led me to try and make amends with those in leadership over me whom I had previously disrespected. I was excited about the future, yet again I was rejected, plus other family issues I have already covered before; I eventually felt thrusted by a series of choices, which landed me in the place where this book was born.

Sometimes those mountain top blessings are meant to sustain us through the difficulties that are just ahead. A desert road that we are not yet capable of recognizing. It's like going to church on Sundays, whether you attend a traditional building service or a fellowship that meets virtually. Sure, it's nice to see friends and fellowship with other believers. Yet, going to church on Sunday should be more about replenishing our strengths and reloading our spiritual weapons so that we may face the rest of the week for the glory of God.

Elijah is surely coming off a magnificent high after standing in faith as THE LORD's representative and utterly putting to shame and even destroying the false prophets and gods of Baal. Yet, he now finds himself in a situation where just the day after this tremendous spiritual victory, he now feels the need to run for his life. Elijah runs clearly into the wilderness, and there he is beautifully ministered to by God and even learns to be so still that in the gentle and quiet whisper, Elijah hears God's voice (1 King 19:12-13 CEB). I came across a quote on a picture the other day from Marianne Williamson that read: "Often miracles are happening right in front of our eyes, but we think they should look different, so we miss them, though they're right there in front of us." Spiritual highs are great, but if we were expecting a different result than what God grants us, we can miss it and actually grow discouraged in our faith.

The events in the life of the Prophet Elijah strike me as Marianne's quote. God is performing amazing miracles left and right of Elijah, and somehow he still ends up in a wilderness experience. It is as if he forgets from one day to the next what God had done for him and through him, and so fear takes over. Perhaps you can relate to this; I certainly can; fear sometimes seems to have greater power over our thoughts than the hope we find in God's promises. Even the hope we have in Christ, the hope that the Holy Spirit reminds us of daily. Yet because things don't look the way we had imagined them to be, or we don't receive the level of hope we were sure we should have received. We dismiss the obvious and miss out completely on God's present blessings.

One thing that has helped me as I have struggled with my own wilderness experience is to live by what I know and not by what I think, just as I've quoted Joyce Meyers before. Meaning I know God loves me. I know He has helped me before; therefore, I do not need to doubt that He will do it again. Even when my faith is weak, or I lose my family, job, or even identity, if I can manage to hold on tight to the knowledge and experience of God in my life, then deep inside, I know that everything will be alright! This is a Godly principle; after all, throughout the Old Testament, God is continually reminding the people of how He saved them from Egypt, surely to get them to understand that if He saved them then, He surely is capable of doing it again!

In the book of 1 Kings, we see this very thing unfolding in the life of Elijah. He is given a difficult task to pronounce God's warning on a truly wicked King. Remember, he was worse than all other kings before him, combined! Not sure if that is what you want to be remembered for, but God had certainly noticed him. My brothers and sisters, the truth is that God is not surprised by our actions. He does not dismiss our disobedience, but He also does not refuses our submission to Him. God stands ready to act on our behalf when the time is right, and we ask Him to. He never forces His will on us, and so He waits. For some of us, we never come to that realization. We fight the work of the Holy Spirit in our lives so much that we refuse to listen when He is whispering in our ears. Elijah, unlike Adam, full of passion, moves in total obedience and proclaims the message of THE LORD, and then God guides him away from the city. Here comes the miracles, ready?

Because God had ordained it, He will now deliver. There will be no rain, no dew, in the city for well over three years! Droughts are usually caused by a diminished or disappearing moisture level in the area. It can be caused by heat, by wind, even by the actions of us mere humans. When we experience droughts, the natural flow of rivers and underground sources affect everything from growing crops to taking care of livestock and animals. Don't forget us humans; we are made of over 70% water. We need it, and we can't go without it. Drought seems to be a reoccurring theme throughout Scripture. In fact, the Promised Land is located on the edge of one of the most immense deserts in the world. The lack of precipitation will often cause these seasons of drought. They have physical implications as well as spiritual ones. I mean, we could say that a wilderness experience is a time of spiritual doubt!

Yet God does not abandon His people nor His evangelist servant Elijah. Immediately after Elijah gives the King the warning of the upcoming drought, God sends him away, gives him water from a brook, and bread plus meat is delivered twice a day from a Raven. I've heard of this delivery service. Your bread and meat delivered in 30 minutes or is free! This alone is a tremendously fantastic thing, the original Grubhub! Eventually, as Elijah is enjoying the provisions of God, the brook he had camped by runs dry, but God shows up again and redirects him across the country to the house of a poor widow. On God's proclamation, the widow cares for the Prophet, while the flower in the pot is never spent and the oil in the jug never runs out. (1 King 17:16 CEB) That's miracle number two! It is almost as if God is preparing Elijah for a future event yet to come where he will need to remember God's goodness in the past. Later on in the Scriptures, Elijah's apprentice Elisha will perform a similar miracle of the endless oil pot! (2 Kings 4 CEB). It sounds like God is in the miracle business. He is always at work in the lives of His faithful servants both to bless them and others around them.

One day, the widow's son dies; this was her only son, her only source of security. Yet Elijah, who has been living rent-free for a couple of years now, seeks God's help on her behalf. The Scriptures tell us that Elijah prays and lays on top of the child and revives him. Miracle number three! Sounds impossible, doesn't it, yet it only does because we refuse to accept it. We cannot admit that God can and will keep His promises when we trust in Him. That is truly what a miracle is, something that seems impossible, yet it happens anyway! Eventually, when over three years had passed during this God-ordained drought, God sends Elijah back to King Ahab to confront him and his 850 prophets. (1 King 18:20-39 CEB). This is truly a monumental battle, one against eight hundred and fifty!

But you see, it is not one against 850 false prophets; it is God, the one true God against 850 false prophets. They don't stand a chance. Elijah once again moves in faith, knowing that he is merely God's instrument, and it will be God who will bring glory to Himself on that day. Elijah arranges for a presentation. He sets up an altar with a bull sacrifice on it, and the prophets of Baal do the same. Then they would both ask their gods to bring rain. In faith, knowing how this whole thing would turn out, Elijah invited the 800 plus prophets to go first. As part of their pagan rituals, they cried out to their gods, hit themselves, whipped themselves, threw themselves into a frenzy really, but nothing happened!

As part of his presentation, Elijah goes a little over the top, but I love how he now begins to mock them when he says, speak louder, maybe your god is sleeping! (Very gutsy of him). After all, it is one man against eight hundred and fifty! But nothing happens; the false prophets cannot bring about a single drop of rain. Elijah then takes his turn and lays down the bull, drenches it in precious water, and even calls for a trench to be dug around his sacrifice and that it be filled with water. Think about this, Elijah is wasting water, or so others might have thought. Yet, he is acting in complete confidence that God will provide as He promised He would, so Elijah prays. "LORD, the God of Abraham, Isaac, and Israel, let it be known today that you are God in Israel and that I am your servant. I have done all these things at your instructions. Answer me, LORD! Answer me so that these people will know that you, LORD, are the real God and that you can change their hearts." (1 Kings 18:36-37 CEB)

Look at what happens next! Then the fire of God fell from Heaven, and it consumes the bull, the wood, the rocks, and the dust. It even licked up the water that had been poured on the bull and in the trench around it. Wow, what a sight, what a demonstration of the one and only God! Notice here that Elijah does not pray for God to show off His great ability or for God to show the people that He was right. God had sent Elijah to preach repentance to these people, and now he prays, LORD, do this so that their hearts may be changed. You see, God is never looking to show what He can do, but He is hoping to change hearts along the way! Elijah ordered that the false prophets be captured immediately, and then he executed each one of them. (1 King 18:40 CEB). I know, kind of dark, but God does not mess around! Our Holy and Just God will ensure that the people understand who supplied their needs, who took care of their oppressors out of their terrible experience, under the rule of an evil King.

Elijah then proclaims to the King to hold a feast in celebration, for he believes the drought will be ending and a storm is coming! Isn't it wonderful when we can speak with full assurance and hope of God's actions to come? Elijah goes up to the mountain and prays again, seeking God's fulfillment of His promise. He sends his servant to the coast to report if any clouds are forming. Eventually, he comes back with a favorable report, and soon enough, the sky darkens with clouds, and the rain begins to fall. Under God's influence and in His power, Elijah seeks the King to show him what the true God of Israel was doing. Unfortunately, he was beaten there by one of the King's advisors.

Interestingly enough, not a day after a great victory, some of us can still wander off into the wilderness and feel abandoned, alone, maybe even forsaken. When Jezebel, the King's evil wife who was truly responsible for Ahab's negative influence with the false prophets, finds out what had taken place, she threatens Elijah's life. Naturally, we could say Elijah runs. In the words of Forest Gump, he ran as fast as his legs could take, heading south towards the kingdom of Judah. But wait, Elijah, stand your ground, remember everything God just did, He will surely take care of you! It doesn't matter, just like Peter took his eyes off Jesus for just a second and lost faith and began to sink, fear took over Elijah. In a moment, as if he was watching a horror film, and something suddenly popped up on the screen, in 1 King 19:3-4 (CEB), we read, "But Elijah ran for His life, he went a day's journey into the wilderness…" There he cries out to God, and he even asked him to die.

What happened to the fearless man of God who took on 850 prophets, who mocked a potential god? Where is the confident, self-assured evangelist servant of the Most High that wasted all that water during his presentation because he knew God would provide, that God would complete the task He had started? I don't know where He is, but I can't help but think about my own life and how a few years back, I too experience a deep faith crisis, and I must admit I felt inconsolable. I was blinded by my fear, by the uncertainty of the future; I could not see what God was doing even though it was right in front of my face. And so I ran from God until one early morning I too cried to the heavens and asked God to take me, I threw in the towel and gave up. Much like Paul, I have always anticipated leaving this earth to be with Christ (Philippians 1:23-24 CEB). However, his was different; this was a complete surrender of life. I honestly did not want to live anymore, and even today, that thought scares me a bit, the fact that I was in such deprived condition that that thought entered my mind. Thank you, LORD, for saving me and rescuing me from that abyss! Thank you for showing me that even when all seems lost, you are still working out your plan of grace and restoration in each of our lives.

As in the case of Elijah, I testify today that God did not give up on me even when I did. I can imagine God as a parent shaking His head in disbelief and maybe a bit of disappointment, saying, oh Elijah, you of little faith. Yet God is always faithful! Because Elijah had been obedient and done what God had previously commanded him to do, he remained steadfast through the many miracles He performed on his behalf. Elijah had stood his ground against impossible odds, God will not abandon Elijah no matter how much faith he may have lost, but will send him one more miracle, and now angels ministered to and fed him. Sounds like what Jesus experienced in His wilderness experience (Matthew 4:11 CEB, more on that later)

Wow!!! First, a raven feeds him, then a poor widow with no food, and now Angels. And yet Elijah is still worried about what little Jezebel has threatened to do to him. How can that be? Maybe you have never experienced such a paralyzing feeling, and perhaps you have never been convinced of what other humans can do to you, so much that it causes you to push God away. I know I have; I don't say that to brag, but to confess my failings and how I have come to miss out on God's comfort at times because I have dared to fear man. Fear you see can amplify our troubles, to make them appear as though they are greater than they are. Scientists tell us that fear is an instinctive human trait or reaction that is supposed to help us run away from danger. That's fine and dandy if it's just you on your own, but when the Almighty God is on our side, fear must not be permitted to reign in us.

On many occasions, God reminds His people to fear not; after all, fear means we don't trust. But if we can learn to trust, we can learn not to fear. Am I making sense here? Sure fear will try to sneak in, but turn those feeling over to God, recount the many ways He has blessed you before, how He has brought you through thus far, and know He will do it again. Don't just think it, recite the very Words of Jesus from the sermon of the mount? "Happy are people who are hopeless because the kingdom of Heaven is theirs. "Happy are people who grieve because they will be made glad. "Happy are people who are humble because they will inherit the earth.

"Happy are people who are hungry and thirsty for righteousness because they will be fed until they are full. "Happy are people who show mercy because they will receive mercy. "Happy are people who have pure hearts because they will see God. (This is truly a Holiness statement! Hebrews 12:14 CEB) "Happy are people who make peace because they will be called God's children. "Happy are people whose lives are harassed because they are righteous because the kingdom of Heaven is theirs. "Happy are you when people insult you and harass you and speak all kinds of bad and false things about you, all because of me. Be full of joy and be glad because you have a great reward in Heaven. In the same way, people harassed the prophets who came before you." (Matthew 5:3-12 CEB)

The trouble is that we often focus on the wrong things. God's miracles are right in front of us, yet we don't allow ourselves to have a broader view. In my darkest of nights, I so turned around, so unfocused that I could not see straight spiritually speaking, and until I came to my senses, I'm sure under the influence of the Holy Spirit, that things began to turn around for the better. That's when I was able to be guided out of my darkness back into the marvelous light of God.

We must take a step back from our troubles, don't focus so much on the negative, but look for that glorious silver living, that glimmer of hope, that small cloud in the sky. Look for the ever gentle voice of God that reassures you as He did with Joshua, I am with you where ever you go, no one will be able to stand up against you, in the same way, I was with Moses, I will be with you, be very brave and strong as you carefully obey all of the instructions. Don't deviate even a bit, then you will have success wherever you go. (Joshua 1:5-9 CEB). What a genuine and effective promise this is; pray it, practice it, believe it, and see how God will help you, how He will come through for you and strengthen you as He did with Elijah!

Eventually, when Elijah stops running, God is able to speak with Him. When we stop and turn to God, then we are ready to reconnect and hear His message of hope again. Almost as if he is forgetting who he is talking to, Elijah proceeds to present his concerns to God, of how afraid he was for his life. In short, he is telling God, sorry, I trusted you to do incredible and amazing feats, but I did not trust you to watch out for little old me. Then God gives him yet another excellent presentation. God causes a great and strong wind to pass by the Prophet, tearing up the mountains and causing rocks to fall, yet God was not in the wind. God then caused the earth to quake, but God was not in the earthquake. A third time God causes a great fire, yet God was not in the fire. And then, as I am sure Elijah is pondering the great forces of nature that he has just witnessed, Scripture tells us that in the sound of a low whisper, Elijah heard God, and Elijah covered himself in humility before God. (1 King 19:9-18 CEB)

How is it possible that after all he had experienced, after all, that God had done through his life, he could still feel so depressed? How is it that he thought running away was best and expected God to come to him in incredible ways that he had perceived in his mind, yet when it doesn't happen, how he thought, he got out of town? Friends, we may end up in a wilderness experience due to our fears leading us to disobey God. Yet, there is never a good enough reason to allow fear to consume us and lead us to forget all that God has done and run for our lives. God always shows up. The maker of the Universe is in the gentleness business. You and I may still expect Him to come charging into our situations and rescue us on a white horse as if we are some sort of damsel in distress. We expect Him to grab the wheel of our cars when we are skidding around for our lives. We anticipate that He will swoosh down from Heaven and save our marriages, our families, our children right when we need it most. All along, we miss His ever gentle voice saying, I love you, and I will always take care of you. Yes, as for the case for many, that care is not always manifested in the way we expect it, but God does have an unchanging, eternal plan for each of us; never doubt that.

For Elijah, once he came out of his runt, and I simply mean, once he began to put his trust in God again, THE LORD led him to anoint the next King, one whom God had chosen. God also led him to meet and train his eventual replacement, Elisha; after all, God was not done ministering to His people. Elijah had done the work he needed to do, and now God will take him. Yes, in the second book of Kings, we see that Elijah is taken up to Heaven in a Chariot of Fire in a whirlwind of air. Perhaps we are not quite ready to go home yet, and maybe you think there is still some good to be done here. Let me say to this that while it may sound righteous to believe such things, never attempt to do a work for God that He has not called you to do. More on that when we cover the life of the Apostle Paul.

On several occasions, we witness Elijah praying, seeking God's guidance. May I suggest we do that same today? No matter where we may be in our wilderness experience, would you just stop for a second, for a minute, for an hour if you can and just be still? THE LORD knows what you need; now just wait on Him to meet you in the middle of your storm. Wait for exactly what He wants you to do, and He will meet your need. I promised you that, based on my own experience, but most notably on the promises of His Word! In the end, God took care of Elijah's enemies as well. King Ahab was killed in battle, and evil Jezebel fell from a tower and was eaten by dogs. Perhaps a fitting end to such great evil. Never doubt God's ability to intervene in the middle of someone else's selfishness and bring something good out of it.

Imagine if we could travel back in time and ask Elijah to share with us what he learned along his wilderness journey, how we too could come to make a difference. I would venture out to say that he might encourage us to always be alert, looking for the right occasion. Never stop relying on God to lead you. Be sure that the fight you are about to pick is the right fight to engage in. Lean on God's previous equipping and move in faith. A Godly perspective will always be fundamental. After all, even the worst of enemies do not measure up to the greatness of the Creator of all things.

LORD, you have promised to be with us, not to abandon us, to take care of our need, to see us through our situation for your honor and glory. Right now, in the middle of my troubles, I realize I simply need to be still. To surrender all my fears, all my problems, and to simply trust in your promises, to trust that you are with me. I am reminded of that faithful chorus: "In this quiet moment, still before your throne, conscious of your presence, knowing I am known. In this quiet moment, set my spirit free! In this quiet moment, in this quiet moment, make a better me." As I learn to practice my trust in you more each day, mold me into the person you have designed for me to be, and help me to be aware of not just the mountain high moments, but of your presence with me, even though the valleys of shadow and death. May your name be praised, LORD, as you teach me the value of trusting and obeying you.

You who have seen me through so many dark nights already. You who have brought me back from the brink of destruction. You who have restored more than I had ever dreamed. Help me to remember that, to focus on your goodness on your blessings. And when trial d come my way to face them head-on knowing not only you are with me, but you go before me. Not only will you strengthen me, but you will fight for me. Let that be my daily hope from this day forth.

Questions to keep exploring.

How can maintaining an attitude of self-development help you take responsibility for your past action?

When was the last time you performed a self-assessment to identify where you may be in your walk with God?

Our spiritual maturity, integrity, and a sense of purpose are all formed in the fire of our trials and tests. How are you reacting to your situations?

Would others agree with you on your description of your behavior during these times?

How have you come to experience God's praise for your actions and His rewards for your faithful activities?

When you face impossible acts, how have you moved in faith rather than run away?

8

NEHEMIAH

Wilderness Experience Caused by Tenacity
and a Desire to Make Things Right.

"The God of heaven will give us success!" I replied. "As
God's servants, we will start building. Nehemiah 2:20 (CEB)

od promises that when we call, He will answer. The
answer to our situations is not found in another Bible
degree or another appointment or another committee,
or even another leadership program. The answer is found in
the amazing grace of God. The Book of Nehemiah is one of my
favorite Scripture characters as it ties so much of God's plan in
the Bible together. You'll see what I mean soon. Nehemiah was
a man living away from his home when God's people were taken
into exile because of their relentless disobedience. Who was
Nehemiah? Supposedly a member of the tribe of Judah, who
caries a rather interesting name which is roughly translated as
God Comforts or Encourages.

This name is significant, because at this point in the story of the people of God, the nation of Israel is basically non-existence, its walls, its source of defense, and the Temple, the place where God promised to dwell with His people, had been destroyed for many years now, and most of the Jewish nation finds itself in exile. Between the Priest Ezra and Nehemiah, it is estimated that approximately 50,000 Hebrews will eventually return home during four separate journeys. During the fourth journey home under the leadership of Nehemiah, we encounter the events of the rebuilding and establishing the presence of Israel back in the Promise Land.

The willful disobedience of the people of God had been so severe that many years before the Kingdom of Israel had been divided. Eventually, God permitted its enemies to overpower them and defeat them. Only three Hebrew kings ruled over the entire united nation; Saul, David, and Solomon. After them, the kingdom was divided into two, the Northern Kingdom (ten tribes) and the Southern Kingdom (two tribes). Eventually, due to a constant string of Kings who did evil in the sight of God, the defeat and destruction of the Northern Kingdom of Israel took place, followed by about a hundred years later the destruction of the Southern Kingdom of Judah. Throughout these events, there are several important Biblical personalities that we must include in these accounts. They serve a continual reminder of the good purpose of God and the eventual re-establishment of the Nation of God.

It is also crucial that we mention these folks as they helped to tie together many of the Old Testament books, bringing us to the clear realization that the Bible is not just a compilation of sixty-six random books. But, it is truly one continuous story of God's grace and His ongoing efforts to bring His creation back into spiritual focus. It also sets biblical events alongside verified secular historical characters, offering validity to the accuracy of God's Word.

First, we have the Prophet Jeremiah, who is also taken into captivity during the final days of Israel's dismantling. During a message from God Himself, which includes the ever-popular Jeremiah 29:11 CEB scriptural promise, just a verse before we have an equally powerful assurance from God. When God says to the people, through Jeremiah, "When seventy years are completed for Babylon, I will come to you and fulfill my good promise to bring you back." Jeremiah 29:10 (CEB) Furthermore, after reminding the people that He indeed has a plan not to harm them but a plan of hope for their future, God also promises the people that when they call on Him, when they pray to Him, that He will listen and in fact when they seek Him, declares THE LORD, with all of their hearts, they will find Him! (Jeremiah 29:12-13 CEB) This is something we can see seventy years later in the accounts of Nehemiah.

Next, we have the powerful visions of the Prophet Ezekiel, who was a contemporary of Jeremiah. Ezekiel was a member of the Priesthood and, therefore, held a higher cultural status than Jeremiah. Nonetheless, they were both sharing God's inspired prophecies of hope with the children of God. God will speak to the people through Ezekiel to bring hope to them in their fallen condition. You see, even in our darkest hours, THE LORD promises to be with us (Psalm 23). As we have mentioned, because of rebellion and disobedience, the children of God have earned themselves what seemed like a one-way ticket to oblivion. Yet, God is always Faithful, and Ezekiel clarifies that God will restore them one day! Ezekiel prophesied beyond just these 70 years. Ezekiel includes an even further prophesy calling for David to be their shepherd. Of course, King David has now been long dead by this time. He was referring then to the line of David that God had promised to establish (2 Samuel 7:8-16 CEB) and our great shepherd yet to come, Jesus Himself (Ezekiel 34:23-24, 37:24 CEB).

The plan of God to return His people to the lands He had

promised to Abraham would now include the rebuilding of the Temple or the place of God's dwelling. This would, of course, set the stage for the coming of Jesus where God reminds them and yes even us, that when He restores all things, He will indeed once again be our God and we will be His people (Ezekiel 37:27 CEB). Ezekiel's prophesy of the people's return includes, of course, the very visual account where God restores the valley of bones to life in the representation of the regenerations and reconstitution of the Nation of Israel (Ezekiel 37).

The next worthy of mentioning would have to be the Prophet, Isaiah. Now, he did serve God much sooner than any of these previously mentioned prophets. Yet, he also prophesied about the return and restoration of Israel. He did so in two parts, one of the actual people and two like Ezekiel years later, in great detail of the coming Messiah (Yashua Ha-Mashiach), who would restore all things according to God's will. In the later chapter of the writings of Isaiah, we find a very condensed jam-packed account of theological teachings in the Bible, way too much to unpack in a few pages here. Yet, for what is worthy of note is the undeniable messages from God through all of these men is what eventually bring us to the accounts of Nehemiah.

The last but not least worthy mention then is Ezra! Ezra was a priest of God, a direct descent from the Levitical lines of Moses and Aaron. Ezra is indeed a contemporary of Nehemiah, and his repatriation efforts for the people back to their ancestral land are equally significant as the events of Nehemiah. Under the Persian King Artaxerxes, Ezra is the first granted permission to come down to Jerusalem with a large company of people. The mission was to rediscover God's law and begin to practice it again. This would include the rebuilding of the Temple. We read in the accounts of Ezra that he gained such success through prayer, intercession, and preaching of God's message of hope. (Ezra 10:9 CEB). One final bonus worthy mention contemporary of Ezra and Nehemiah would be the Prophet Malachi, who wrote the final book in the Old Testament.

It is interesting to note how God will use the most unlikely people to accomplish His will. The events here occur in a very tumultuous time and geographical area where the Mighty Assyrian Empire in the 8th Century BC conquered and destroyed Israel's Northern Kingdom. One hundred plus years later, King Nebuchadnezzar of Babylon defeated the Assyrians and eventually conquered Judah's Southern Kingdom and destroyed the Temple and the City Walls in 586 BC. This was followed by the eventual defeat of the Babylonians by the Persian Emperor Cyrus the Great, who decreed the Jewish people's initial return to the land of Israel and the rebuilding of the Temple of God.

Cyrus was followed by other Kings, including King Darius, which brings us to Daniel's Biblical accounts and the lion's den (Daniel 6 CEB) plus Shadrach, Meschach, and Abednego in the firefly furnace. Eventually, we arrive at King Xerxes (yes, the same King we see in the movie 300, who conquered even the mighty Spartans and the rest of the Greeks). Xerxes was the husband of Queen Esther, whom you might remember helped save the Jewish people from complete annihilation (Esther 5). After he came his son King Artaxerxes whom we already mentioned, and under whom the final return of the Jewish people is orchestrated and completed by Nehemiah.

Nehemiah was an important man, the cupbearer to the King! This was a significant position of status and trust as it was their duty to safeguard the King's wine and food against possible poisoning. Nehemiah would have been personally known and held in high esteem by the Persian King Artaxerxes. As we have seen already Queen Esther, may have had a hand in all that took place here. Her husband Xerxes was brutally assassinated by his bodyguard, giving rise to Artaxerxes, his son. This makes Esther either his mom or at least someone who the child Artaxerxes grew up around. Maybe this is another good reason why King Artaxerxes looks upon Ezra's and now Nehemiah's request with such favor. Nehemiah, moved by the visit of a man from Jerusalem and his report of its decrepit state of the wall in Israel, enters a time of mourning and personal confession (Nehemiah 1:4-11 CEB) that eventually gets him noticed by the King. No doubt, under the leading of God, the King grants Nehemiah permission to travel to Israel and rebuild its walls! Nehemiah not only asks the Kings for his blessing to go but also for his help with materials, which the King grants. Most importantly, first and foremost, we read in Nehemiah 1 that Nehemiah seeks the guidance, favor, and intervention of God. Always the best place to start!

Once again, it is curious that even after the exile, there are still those even in a foreign land who hold onto their faith in a truly benevolent God (THE LORD). Not only that, but Nehemiah takes it upon himself to acts as a mediator, even a high priest of sorts, before God when he seeks the forgiveness of his sin and that of Israel (Nehemiah 1:6 CEB). He even recalls the promises of God and prays according to them, expecting God to keep His Word and return the remnants of Israel to their Promised Land. By this time, remember Ezra had already made three trips back to the Holy Land and brought quite a few Jews back with him, but it will be Nehemiah's final journey that will seal the deal if you will. Ezra brought back the law and rebuilt the Temple (Ezra 5:1-6:15 CEB), now Nehemiah is tasked by God to rebuild the city's defenses, its outer wall.

I have learned a few things in my wilderness journey, and one of those is that it is ok to seek the help of others and believe that God is playing the long game, and as a result, He will always fulfill His promises. After receiving the King's blessings, plus the material needed to complete the task. Nehemiah heads down south on a very long journey and soon discovers that even when you try to do the right thing. There will always be those who will try to discredit you, intimidate you, and try to force you into what they call the company line instead of letting you accomplish what God is calling and guiding you to do.

I remember times towards the beginning of what I have identified as the early days of my wilderness experience; this was the case for me. I was so mixed up with what others expected of me and what I believed God wanted me to do that it often manifested itself as frustration. At times blowing up with unkind words towards those who I'm sure thought they were doing me a favor by intervening somehow. If anyone knows this secret to life is me, never attempt to explain your position or take a stand against someone who has already made up their mind about you or your plans. Simply humble yourself, practice the spiritual discipline of keeping your mouth shut (Job 13:5 CEB), and walk away from that person or organization if necessary, trusting that God is ultimately in control. Can He use others to get you to slow down a bit when necessary? Of course, He did so with the Apostle Paul when he wanted to go into Asia, yet the Spirit prevented him (Acts 16:6 CEB). Can God even use the stubbornness of others to save you from making a terrible mistake possibly! Absolutely, He used a jackass to get the false Prophet Balaam to come to his senses (Numbers 22:21-39 KJV).

When times are rough, it is human nature to blame others, make excuses, and simply justify our actions due to the unkindness of others. Sadly, I certainly practiced these misguided efforts during my journey. Yet, if we genuinely believe that God is sovereign, then why can't we believe that God can use all things for His good? Even the selfish and stubborn actions of those who professionally abuse us and try to hinder our drive to do what we believe is right. Like Nehemiah, we must come to God in prayer and know He will see us through our troubles (Psalms 46 CEB). No matter how difficult things may become, remember the words of Paul and the Prophet Nahum as they encourage their readers not to grow weary and lose heart (Hebrew 12:3 CEB) but to hold onto God's promises knowing without a doubt that "THE LORD is good, a haven in a day of distress. He acknowledges those who take refuge in Him." (Nahum 1:7 CEB)

Through Nehemiah's prayer in Chapter One, we learn that he was concerned about the problem of Jerusalem's desolation. Eventually, we find out that Nehemiah journeyed back to Jerusalem and discovered the full scope of the situation. We can make two preliminary observations: One, chapter 3 reveals Nehemiah's extraordinary gift of administration and organization. He was able to mobilize and empower forty-four separate groups of people for the ingenious task of rebuilding the walls. And two, this passage shows how people working together can accomplish more than if it was just one person trying to do all the work. The biblical principle is this: every believer, everyone who calls themselves a Christian, a child of God, must be involved in ministry because everyone has a job to do and a part to play. How then does your wilderness experience cause you to examine what your God-given gifts are and how you can mobilize others by utilizing them for His glory?

.   It's hard to find the right job, isn't it? Especially in today's economy. Nonetheless, there is a lot to be done, and the available job may not be our first preference but are necessary tasks that must be completed so that our society may continue to function. Some may be doing exactly what they need to be doing, while others may be struggling to find their niche. I am speaking of both in the secular setting and our spiritual callings. It might help us all feel better if we hear someone else's job history. Listen to these:

- My first job was working in an orange juice factory, but I got canned because I couldn't concentrate.
- I studied a long time to become a doctor, but I didn't have any patience.

- I became a professional fisherman but discovered that I couldn't live on my net income.
- After many years of trying to find steady work, I finally got a job as a historian until I realized there was no future in it.

Ok, ok, these are terrible dad jokes, but I hope they made you smile, but most importantly, I hope they made you think about God's faithfulness and provisions in your own life. As I found myself neck-deep in my own wilderness experience, I could not find work. Even with my educational background and experience, I could not get anyone to call me back. Finally, Walmart called and hired me as a part-time cashier. I must confess I was devastated. I did not want to work for Walmart; I felt I was above that somehow. Yet I humbled myself and went to work. From this basic position, God has seen it fit to provide for our family as He quickly helped me move up the leadership ladder. Going from cashier to managing the front end and working as a Training Coordinator to eventually becoming an Assistant Manager all under three years. As of the writing of these pages, God has provided yet again, with a new promotion where now I work in an area of the company where we train new managers.

Furthermore, I can see how all those years ago, when I started with this company, how God made sure our family would be provided for in the future yet to come. As we lived through the Covid pandemic, I became an essential worker all of a sudden. For those perhaps like me who would look down on this organization, I can testify that Walmart has been good to me and generous in its support of the abilities and talents God developed in me in previous ministry jobs. Through them, God has provided the means for us to purchase a new Hooke, raise our children and have the free time to enjoy the beauty of Florida fully. I am truly thankful. God knows best, and He will always provide for His people. Trust in His will for your life, even if it's not as glamorous as you would want it to be.

As we can read in chapter 3 of the book of Nehemiah, our protagonist has his work caught out for him. From the comforts of being the King's cupbearer to getting down and dirty on a building project. Together with the wall workers, they accomplished an incredible task as they set a world record for teamwork. Nehemiah was able to build his team around a central rallying point. He pointed them to the purpose of the work, which is the glory of God. Think about why you do what you for God? Whatever that may be. Are you doing it just because you are good at it, because you are the best person for the position, maybe because no one else will do it? Or do you do it for the glory of God? Before you answer, let me remind you that God knows our hearts, and He does remind us that, by our fruits, others will know who we belong to. (Matthew 7:15-20 CEB).

The people of God longed for God's city to regain its splendor and for God to get the credit. And soon, God will bless them with their heart's desire. We, too, should long for the same thing in our service to God, no matter what wilderness we may be traveling to. To put God first will always help us focus on what is essential and hopefully bring us through our journey of faith development. Even while at Walmart, I have shared my faith with dozens of people and share with all of my associates regarding God's goodness in my life. You see, the purpose of all ministry, and really of life itself, is to give glory to God. 1 Corinthians 10:31 (CEB) puts it concisely: "So whether you eat or drink or whatever you do, do it all for the glory of God."

This is evident by where Nehemiah decides to begin the rebuilding project. In chapter 3, we read that "Eliashib the high priest and his fellow priests went to work and rebuilt the Sheep Gate." It is no accident that the list starts at the Sheep Gate. It's another way of saying, "Put God first." How do I know this? This gate provided easy access to the Temple and was given this name because all the sheep that entered through it went to be sacrificed. Nehemiah establishes that their relationship with

God will be primary by beginning here. As they rebuild, as they hope for the future, as they come together to recreate the glory of God, they will put God first and in the center, and my friends, so must we!

We must make sure we are dedicated to God before we begin working for Him; otherwise, our labor will be in vain. When we are traveling through a difficult time or see an impossible task ahead, drawing near to the source of grace, the creator of all things will be the only move to make. God, you see, is not impressed with our more labor. He simply wants our hearts. That's why worship must always precede our works. This is also why God sent Ezra down to Jerusalem first, to rediscover the Word of God and reestablish the practice of worshiping God. For the sake of this chapter, I like to draw upon the behaviors and actions of Nehemiah and identify six principles that I pray will help each of us not only learn to work well with others but also trust in God when we can't see a way out of our situation. Whether we go about the business of God or as we recommit ourselves to the mission of His purpose, even if we are currently in a bit of a spiritual funk. Leaning on God and others will prove to be a wellspring of strength for us in these dark days. We must then begin with:

1) Leaders must set the example.

As we just pointed out, the high priest had no hesitation using his consecrated hands to swing a hammer or push a wheel barrel! As befitted the superior dignity of his office, he wore a sacred garment, and yet, here he was picking up rubble and laying bricks. Are you a leader of anything at your work, school, or community? Why not? No one has asked you, you say, no opportunities to take on a role? Or perhaps you just don't know how to get involved, or maybe you think you have nothing to offer? If this is the case, I hope you have been examining your life throughout this book and hopefully now have a better self-image of who you are in God's eyes. Whether you have the world's most remarkable talent or not, there is always something to do! We are all called to lead in one way or another. We just need to seek that purpose and develop it in our walk with God!

If you do see yourself as a leader of some sort, the question for you then is, do you lead those in your care by example? Do you get involved? This is often referred to as servant leadership. Do you serve others or expect them to serve you? (Mark 10:45 CEB). Do you live your life in obedience to God or just doing your own thing? If you do, great; if not, please take a moment even now to identify why you may not and make it right. Friends, if we hope to get out of our spiritual rut, we must always be willing to commit to being involved with our time, our talents, our treasures in the work of God, all without excuses, as we experience the leading of the Holy Spirit in our lives. How can I be so sure of this?

2) God uses all kinds of people.

In verse 8 of Nehemiah chapter 3, we read how a goldsmith and then a perfume maker made repairs on the wall. THE LORD didn't need a thousand masons and carpenters to rebuild the wall he needed ordinary people who were willing to work. There was a place for everyone and a job for everyone to do. That's the beauty of gift-based ministry. God has gifted each of us and called each of us to be involved in a lifestyle of servanthood. Involved in a ministry that He has prepared for us all. We need to step forward and be counted; otherwise, we will never achieve our full potential.

I get it; we have been burned or emotionally scared by others who have abused us and taken advantage of us, so we do tend to become jaded, and it can seem impossible to proclaim, here I am, LORD send me. I know, I have been there, yet that is precisely what we must get to a place of being able to do. God will prepare us as He calls us rather than merely calling those already prepared. I am not saying it won't happen, but God is waiting for you and for me, regardless of our professional abilities, to go and be His hands and feet of grace to a world in need. The choices is ours to get involved or not. Even in our darkest nights of the soul, as we feel useless with low self-esteem, God wants to use us. After all from Nehemiah, we also learn that:

3) Some people will simply not work.

There is a place for everyone and a job for everyone to do. Yet, there will always be those who refuse to exert themselves. We see this in verse 5: "The next section was repaired by the men of Tekoa, but their nobles would not put their shoulders to the work under their supervisors." They did not want to follow orders. They were too proud to submit themselves to the supervisors of the job. Because they were nobles, they thought themselves better than others. I hope this is not your perspective. The Word of God is clear that we are not to think of ourselves as better than anyone else but humble ourselves before God. (Philippians 2:3 CEB)

The phrase "would not put their shoulders to the work" suggests that it was pride more than anything else which kept them from pitching in. What form of pride is stopping you from being the compassionate person God needs you to be? We should love doing the work of God because we believe it makes a kingdom impact. Some of the happiest Christians are those who are serving in their area of giftedness. On the other hand, some of the grumpiest Christians are those who are "pew potatoes" and are not willing to put their shoulder to the efforts at hand. We can all identify who these persons are, and if you cannot, then maybe you are that person. This is not a criticism by any means, but hopefully an eye-opening exercise. No one is above service; even Jesus, being equal with God, did not consider equality with Him something to grasp and yet humbled Himself even to the point of death on a cross (Philippines 2:5-8 CEB). We have to be humble before God and not proud. After all, God stands against the proud but favors the humble (James 4:6 CEB). We must be counted on the side of those willing to get involved for the glory of God, as we see in the fourth principle I like to share.

4) Some actually will do more work.

I believe this is mainly because of those who will not humbly take their post. During the 2020 pandemic, many of my coworkers would not come to work during the great scare of the coronavirus. Yet we were considered essentials; therefore, our doors never closed, and as we were one of the few places available for people to go and have some human interaction. Because we experience high absences in our workforce, the rest of us had to do more than expected to cover for others so that we might still have a job the next day. Sometimes there can be a valid reason for not showing up to work, yet most times, the reasons are selfish, which is what is happening here. Because some people refused to work on the wall project, others had to step up and fill in. And they gladly did!

According to the accounts of Nehemiah 3, such were the men from Tekoa! When they finished their work, they went on to work on another section. The men of Binnui did the same thing in verses 18 and 24 of our story. Furthermore more we can read earlier in verse 21: "Meremoth repaired another section, from the entrance of Eliashib's house to the end of it." After he finished his assignment, he worked on the wall in front of his neighbor's house. There's a tendency within most of us to complete the work we volunteered for or the work that we are tasked with and then stop, stretch out our arms and say, "wasn't it great to do THE LORD's work? Thank God I'm finished now."

But not so with these men. They knew that kingdom work is never finished. When we complete one task for THE LORD, we can't sit back and think we've fulfilled our ultimate responsibility as a Christian. Friends, as long as there are lost souls, hungry children, abused women, imprisoned men, confused adolescents, there is work for us to do. Think about what you are going through, and hopefully, those who are speaking hope into your life. It is your turn now to speak hope into the lives of others. As you are counted as God's humble labor force, learn the joy and passion of serving God and your fellow man. We must truly learn to go above and beyond for the glory of God. Our fifth principle shows us how some did just that and how their enthusiasm led them to work even harder.

5) Some work with passion.

In this entire chapter, there is only one guy mentioned who worked zealously. If we look at verse 20, we read, "Next to him, Baruch zealously repaired another section…". The Hebrew word for zealously means "to burn or glow" and suggests that Baruch burned a lot of energy. He was not just serving; he was on "fire." Are you willing to go the extra mile and burn with zeal and passion in your service of God and others? This will not be achievable in your strength. You must seek and rely on God's encouragement. I have discovered in my journey that there is no better way to get me out of my own head than when I focus on the needs of others and get moving to help them. I am sure we can all do a little more if we moved in faith! What is it that you are passionate about? Your faith, your family, your future?

We need that internal fire to get us going, don't we? Not just our passion but most importantly, God's Holy Spirit! There is an old hymn that calls on God to send the fire today! Send it we pray LORD, and grant us your vision and passion for getting to work right where you have us. Even through our sadness and loneliness, or depression and sense of worthlessness, grant us LORD opportunities to witness to others of your compassion. The good news is that we are not alone in this effort! No, not only is God with us, but He always provides other people in our lives that we can lean on. This is our final principle from Nehemiah's actions!

6) Some worked as communities!

We read in chapter 3 that this took place either on a section in front of their home or on another section away from their neighborhood. Many worked and repaired the portions of the wall that were nearest to their own homes. If we followed this example, our neighborhoods would look a lot differently. We must look at our neighbors as our primary mission field. Befriend them. Serve them. Pray for them and share Christ with them by our actions of love and kindness. And then bring them to church and get them involved doing the same for others! As a body of believers, we must be committed to making an impact in our cities, in our counties, in our countries, and the rest of the world. But, it's got to first begin at home. In John 15:16 CEB, Jesus told his disciples that He had appointed them to go and bear fruit. The word "appointed" means that He had "strategically placed them." The critical truth that emerges is this: God has placed each of us strategically right where he needs us to be. Yes, even during my wilderness journey, I have been able to look back at my life and recognize the prevenient grace of God at work in me and through me to bless others.

God appoints, and you and I must simply commit to follow Him and do as instructed. If God's work will continue to get done, if we are going to continue to develop our faith in Him, and if we are going to reach new lost souls for His kingdom, we're called to cooperate with one another. We must keep the main thing the main thing, as they use to say, by never forgetting that God's glory is at stake. We might not all give equally, but we can all make equal sacrifices in the eyes of God. We can all create equal opportunities for others to come to Jesus. To work well with others on a much bigger job than we will demand everything we have, we need to recognize these six principles.

You see, I believe Nehemiah understood that everyone that was working had their own troubles, concerns, and fears, yet when they came together under the same mission, it gave them all-purpose and direction. This doesn't mean that their troubles were simply banished, but this new aspiration granted them a new perspective and clarity of their situation. This allowed them to rise above it for the greater good of the community and their neighbors. Have you heard the story or ever noticed how geese tend to fly in a V-formation? Geese often cover thousands of miles before reaching their destination and they can only get to where they're headed if they work together.

Scientists tell us that by flying as they do, the members of the flock create an upward air current for one another. By flying in a V-formation, scientists again claim that the whole flock gets 71% greater flying range than if each goose flew on its own. When one goose gets sick or wounded, two fall out of formation with it and follow it down to help and protect it. They stay with the struggler until he's able to fly again. The geese in the rear of the formation are the ones who do the honking. It's their way of announcing that they're following and everything's going well. The repeated honks encourage those in front to stay the course and carry on. It is the instinct of geese to work together to accomplish the ultimate distant goal of migration.

Friends, it must be our instinct to work side by side as well. Whether it's flapping, helping, or simply honking and encouraging, we are in it together as a flock of believers. This will enable us to accomplish what we set out to do. Let God use your spiritual journey to motivate others, and equally, you find encouragement in the journey of others. The life of Nehemiah reminds us that if we are to move along with our lives and God's purpose, we must recommitting ourselves afresh every day to the mission He calls us to live out, where ever we may be. We will need to work together and always remember that all that we do is for the glory of God. Nehemiah faced other threads and difficulties, yet he remained closed to the source of strength, God. And God saw him through it with success!

Some may prefer to merely honk, some may prefer to flat their wings, and others may lean more towards helping the needy, and you know that's ok with me, as long as it brings glory to God and His church benefits spiritually, in maturity and yes in attendance as we. All working together to simply bring glory to our Father in heaven, who has saved us, called us and placed us right where we need to be from this day forth. Can you believe that? My dear reader, I am but your bother, your servant! While I get to pen down what God has instructed me in this book, my experiences lead me to live in the assurance of God's perfect timing, but my calling is no different than yours. To preach His Word and to serve those in need. This is the call of every believer, and together we can make a real difference. Together we can lift each other and be a source of support and strength.

Sometimes we think people are out to get us, and most of the time is just natural human paranoia. Yet there are those times when we know factually that people mean to hurt us, to derail us, to damage our spiritual wholeness in any way they can. In the end, it is not so much that they succeed as much as we give them power over us because we allow fear to overtake us. We become a self-fulfilling prophesy and make those things come true. I've spent too much time blaming others for what my wife and I were going through in my journey. Only focusing on those who may or may not have genuinely sought to hurt us, that I lost myself in my self-pity, in my depravity, and I only ended up digging a deeper hole for myself. If we are to break the cycle of our depression of our wilderness encounters, of our dependency on others, then let us trust in God as Nehemiah did and let us proclaim together: "The God of heaven will make us prosper" (Nehemiah 2:20 CEB).

If Nehemiah was sitting by you right now, what would you ask him? If it were me, I would ask for some nuggets of wisdom for facing impossible odds. I would picture him telling me to allow the challenges in my life to motivate me to reach higher for God's glory. To always look ahead, plan, and set a vision that all can follow. Be ready to move according to the guidance of God and his purpose. Go fast and go hard; do not be afraid, for THE LORD is with you! Yet be quick to listen for His voice and be willing to slow down and or give it your all if and when required!

Yes, we will have troubles in this world. Yes, we will be persecuted, but fear not for Jesus has already won the day, lean on Him, lean on each other and move forward to fulfill God's purpose and do that which we know is the right thing to do, serve one another in God's name and in total obedience accomplish the will of God right where He has appointed us to be. The wall that was my life was destroyed by the sin I allowed to consume me. Yet after a time of separation both from my wife and ministry, God called us back together and began to rebuild us. We first sought Him to worship Him together, and then He prepares us and has now launched us out in His service. I pray you may find truth in the life of Nehemiah and that perhaps my own journey may be of encouragement to you, that God never leaves us but truly goes before us.

Questions to keep exploring.

When was the last time you checked in on your neighbors?

How can you show the love of God to your community by the way you live your life?

Is there something you can do for your neighbor that will make them wonder about the hope in you?

Where and how is God calling you to express your hope in Him right where you are right now?

What fears must you still submit to God that you may find the strength to focus on His purpose for your life?

Is there a team you could join to help you find success in your labor for God?

How can focusing on the needs of others help you to get out of your wilderness experience and learn to be blessed by the good gifts of God in the lives of those around you?

9

JESUS

A Preordained Wilderness Experience Directed by Godly
Promise to Restore Creation to Its Rightful Place!

In accordance with God's established plan and
foreknowledge, He was betrayed. Acts 2:23 (CEB)

A m I really about to compare my life experience with that of the Son of God? Well, yes, but let me explain. The connection I will seek to make will be related to the humanity of Jesus, certainly not His divinity. Laying aside the miraculous way Jesus the man came into our plane of existence, there is clear evidence in Scripture regarding Jesus' claim as a member of the homo sapien species. The Gospel, according to Luke, points out how He grew physically and intellectually (Luke 2:40, 52 CEB). We know, of course, that He ate, slept, grew tired, bled, and died on a cross due to His injuries. (John 4:6-7; 19:28-42 CEB). Even after His resurrection, He again ate, drank, and even allowed others to see and touch His physical scars (Luke 24:39-43 CEB). Because Jesus was human, He could certainly relate to the pain that such a reality brings. Disappointments, betrayal, lies, and even the intentional abuse of others. If Jesus' humanity shows us one simple thing, the human journey may require us to suffer. Such suffering may not always be obvious, yet unless we seek to find its meaning, it will only make it more painful.

Yet Jesus teaches us another crucial lesson about suffering: although pain may come, the only place to be in the midst of it all is close to the Father. When we grow closer to God and trust Him more than the lies the enemy will cast our way, then our focus will shift from our troubles, from our negative situations back to the loving plan of God. He who says, you are my child, whom I love so much, is always with us, especially in the hard times. But why would God allow suffering to come our way in the first place? Why did He allow His son to suffer so much more? The obvious answer is that we live in an evil world where too many people take it upon themselves to harm others through the blessing of free choices. Now I know this is not a good reason, yet it is the reality of things. Still, an even better answer would be because He loves us, of course (John 3:16 CEB). And because He loves humanity, He gave up His son to pay the debt we owed, that we might not die but live for eternity in Him. What an extraordinary faithful act that proves God's promises can be trusted!

But was there not another possible way? I don't think so. In the times of Noah, we are told that every intention and thought of the human heart was only towards evil (Genesis 6:5 CEB). It seems like we are back there again, yet, only God can pay the price He requires. Even the best human beings fall short of the purity of the spotless Lamb of God. Who will require atonement for their sins and continual disobedience towards God. Think of your own life, your own experiences; if lessons were easy to learn, why do we keep making silly mistakes? If God calls us His friends (John 15:15 CEB), if He for thousands of years has been trying to restore us to Him, why do we still reject His sovereignty and often disregard His providential guidance over our lives as we choose to go at it alone? It seems to me that even amid our perdition, which we often bring upon ourselves, the only way we seem to learn is to experience hardship. Unfortunately, this is true, and if you don't believe me look at children. How many times do parents try to save their kids from making mistakes, only to have those kids go and trip over the same stones? I surely was one of those; I don't say that with pride but with a bit of regret. How I wished I had listened to my parents more when I was younger!

I know it doesn't seem to make too much sense to our wayward minds. Still, if we are willing to trust in the complete plan of God, then perhaps just like Shadrach, Meschahk, and Abednego did, when we face the symbolic fiery ovens of life, may we may proclaim loyalty to God alone. Rather than give up on the understanding of His provision and safety even in the midst of possible actual death. (Daniel 3:16-20 CEB.) Jesus the Christ was no different; He knew death and suffering through the atoning of His blood was the only way to pay the price our sin required, and still, He went to the cross for us! Knowing that suffering may be necessary should not stop us from remaining faithful to God. Knowing that He will indeed see us through it should definitely encourage us to stay the course and keep moving forward.

In the Gospel, according to Matthew, chapter 4, we have the account of Jesus' own wilderness experience. If you have ever doubted whether God will allow such times in our lives or even lead us where we will live through such hurtful times, see here what His own Son endured. In chapter 4, verse 1, we read that the Spirit led Jesus into the wilderness that the devil might tempt Him. No, I know I have said before that the devil doesn't make us do anything, and that's true, but he certainly offers whispers of temptations that if we give in to them, will cause us to sin by our own actions. Jesus' account seems so familiar to what Job initially went through, don't you think? Jesus, who was living in Heaven, enjoying His Godhood, willingly comes down to live in the wilderness, a life of suffering and rejection. After being cleansed through a ceremonial baptism, it officially all begins here, and then Jesus willingly enters a time of testing. Much like in our own settings, please notice that Jesus is not alone, for the Spirit is with Him!

Our wilderness times will often bring doubt to our mind where we will question our faith in God and our belief in His reality. Even leading us to emotional outbreaks that would otherwise be counter to our day-to-day behaviors. God is with you in the middle of your trials; believe it! Yet never doubt, for doubt in God's plan will undoubtedly lead us to FAIL: Fear, Anxiety, Insubordination, and Loafing. Instead, trust in God's design and allow His Holy Spirit to develop in us: Healing, Obedience, Perseverance, Empowerment. While Jesus' events do not include a faith crisis, the devil certainly tries to get Him to question His relationship with the Creator. Jesus' wilderness experience required some severe time of fasting and meditation, forty days to be exact. Scripture tells us that right when Jesus was starving (a clear human experience, by the way), the tempter came to Him.

As I think of my Christian walk, especially the last ten years or so, I have often identified my own times of spiritual weakness directly related to times when I have been less than practical or effective in my relationship with God. As I look back at my life, when my relationship with my wife began to fall apart, I can see now that my relationship with God was also very weak. Those times when I have neglected my Savior, grown content of His love, or even foolishly disregarded His grace, and those are the times when I have fallen into sin by giving in to the temptation I had experience in those specific situations. However, with God's help, I have learned to reconnect with Him, in prayer, through Scripture reading, and overall times of solitude. (We can call that the Jesus Model!)

Maybe for you, your wilderness experience is a time of silence in your walk with God. It is a season of uncertainty, unanswered prayers, banishment, isolation, persecution, uncertainty, impossibility, suffering, shame, or maybe a time of incredible transformation, where the end result is unclear. We have plenty of examples of this in the Bible. This is really what this book is all about, examining the wilderness experiences of others in hopes of finding a correlation between their journey and ours. So that we may identify what gave them hope, and attempt to hold on to that very hope for our own spiritual maturing, that we may avoid ongoing spiritual backsliding. In times of war, sometimes soldiers are called to take significant risks, sometimes risks that will certainly result in death. However, for the benefit of the greater good, many brave men and women have taken on these types of missions throughout history, and many have died to help their side and have a better chance at victory.

In the book of Romans chapter 8 in the Bible, we read that we are more than conquerors in our trials and tribulations through Christ who loved us. Think about that? Because of Christ volunteering to make the ultimate sacrifice, you and I are victorious. Talk about another great promise from God! Just like those soldiers I've told you about, Jesus willingly took on the most significant risk ever, which resulted in His death. He knew that was the end, and still, He did it! Well, it would not be a finite end. When Jesus is born, we could say that's really when His trial began. Remember the story of His birth? King Harrod wanted to kill Him, talk about persecution. Things were so bad that his family had to flee to Egypt. Eventually, Jesus grows up, becomes a man, and lives happily ever after, right? Yeah, not really!

In the Gospel of Mark chapter one, we see a description of these humble beginnings: "The beginning of the good news about Jesus Christ, God's Son... (Did you know Good News is also translated as Gospel?) In Verse 4, John the Baptistiser was in the wilderness. He was calling for people to be baptized to show that they were changing their hearts and lives and wanted God to forgive their sins." This is a great imagery. John is in the wilderness calling people. Why are people even there? Because we all go through wilderness experiences, according to what I've explained from the beginning. They are literally in the middle of nowhere. I had the privilege to visit this location by the Jordan River, and it's out there, in relationship to the City of Jerusalem and even Galilee. Let's carry on to verse 9 in Mark 1: "About that time, Jesus came from Nazareth of Galilee, (which is north of there) and John baptized Him in the Jordan River." Wait, what was Jesus doing in the wilderness? You will see. "While He was coming up out of the water, Jesus saw Heaven splitting open and the Spirit, like a dove, coming down on Him. And there was a voice from Heaven: "You are my Son, whom I dearly love; in you, I find happiness." At once, the Spirit of God forced Jesus out into the wilderness. He was in the wilderness for forty days, tempted by Satan. He was among the wild animals, and the Angels took care of Him."

Friends, you may not like the current situation you may be going through, but I want you to understand that wilderness experiences are not meant to keep us down. No, they are intended to prepare us for what God has in store for our future. Jesus is led into this time of temptation by the Spirit Himself. Wow! Perhaps God has led you in to your time of trials because He knows what a great and faithful follower will come out of these life pressures. Remain faithful though it all! Let us read the last part of verse 13 again. Was He alone? Did God abandon Him? No, we read that the Angels took care of Him! One of my favorite Scripture verses comes from the book of Joshua. After Moses died and Joshua took over, leading over two million people into a new land, into an unknown wilderness, God came to Joshua and said, you are in charge, good luck, I hope it all works out!? No, God said cross the river and take the people into the land I have promised them.

Then God says in Joshua 1:5-9 (CEB), check this out...maybe sensing a bit of hesitation on Joshua's face, God says: "Joshua, no one will be able to stand up against you during your lifetime. I will be with you in the same way I was with Moses. I won't desert you or leave you. Be brave and strong because you are the one who will help this person take possession of the land, which I pledged to give to their ancestors. Be very brave and strong as you carefully obey all of the instructions that Moses, my servant, commanded you. Don't deviate even slightly from it, either to the right or left. Then you will have success wherever you go."

Do you recall the story of Jesus in the wilderness while the devil tempted Him? (Matthew 4:1-11 CEB). We know that the devil came and offered different temptations, including physical needs and the opportunity to be selfish rather than selfless, to misuse the gifts and talents God bestowed on all believers. And finally, a temptation of vanity or rebellion against God's sovereignty over our lives. How did He defend Himself? By using the Word of God. Jesus always responded to the devil by saying, "For it is written..." What did God tell Joshua to do? To not depart from the law that Moses had given them. The law being the Word of God. Even Jesus quoted the same law in His wilderness experience.

The secret then, to keep in mind to endure and surpass our times of wilderness experience, and yes, they will come to every faithful believer, is to stay close to God, to His Word, to His promises. Are you feeling alone? Then God promises to be with you, to never leave you or forget you. (Joshua 1:9 CEB). You or your family have financial struggles? You need a job real bad? God promises to provide for all of our needs according to His riches, not yours, in glory. (Philippians 4:19 CEB.) Feeling abandoned, like no one cares, God promises that because He loves us so much that He would send His Son so that whoever believes in Him will live eternally in fellowship with Him. (John 3:16 CEB.)

Yet Jesus' wilderness roller coaster ride it's not over. We could spend hours talking about it, yet let us simply fast forward to the end. It's almost time for Jesus to fulfill what He came to do, which is to die on the cross. To take on death and eternal separation from God itself so that we never have to. We then arrive at what we call the garden experience. Do you remember what happened there? Let's read in the Gospel according to Luke on chapter 22:39-46 (CEB): "Jesus left and made His way to the Mount of Olives, as was His custom, and the disciples followed Him. When they arrived, He said to them, "Pray that you won't give in to temptation." Then He withdrew from them about a stone's throw, knelt, and prayed. "Father, if it's your will, take this cup of suffering away from me." Do you think Jesus the man truly wanted to do this? Listen to His prayer! He is hoping for a way out but ultimately recognizes that God is in control as He proclaims, however, not my will but Your will be done."

Then look at what happens again; an Angel appeared to Him and strengthened Him. The same thing that happened after the devil tempted Him in the wilderness! The same thing that happened with the prophet Isaiah! The same thing that I believe God did for me in my darkest hour when I felt His presence closer than ever before. So you think your situation is complicated? Look how bad it was for Jesus. He was in anguish and prayed even more earnestly. His sweat became like drops of blood falling on the ground. Science tells us that when one is under severe stress, the capillaries or the small veins in our heads can burs. When Jesus got up from his arduous prayer time, He goes back to the disciples. He found them asleep, overcome by grief. He said to them, "Why are you sleeping? Get up and pray so that you won't give in to temptation." What is another secret to not fall into the temptations that comes our way? Pray. Get up and pray so that you won't give in to temptation.

Fast forward one last time, Jesus is on the cross, He has already been beaten, completely humiliated, painfully rejected by His friends, including the Apostle Peter and the others and now the sin of the world, pass, present, and future, yes even the bad choices that you and I still practice, were poured upon His shoulder. It was so bad that Jesus proclaims, "My God my God, why have you forsaken me? Jesus had always had a perfect connection with the Father above, and now because of the sin upon Him, God himself could not look at His Son, and Jesus felt that anguish, that despair, that separation, that loss. Eventually, naturally, Jesus dies (so human of Him!) Still, then as it is always the case for the children of God, His wilderness experience comes to an end when He rises from death victorious.

Because of what's Christ did, you and I are victorious in our situations as we allow the Holy Spirit to lead us, so much so that the Apostle Paul says to the church in Rome. Romans 8:16-17 (CEB) "All who are led by God's Spirit are God's sons and daughters You didn't receive a spirit of slavery to lead you back again into fear, but you received a Spirit that shows you are adopted as his children. With this spirit, we cry, "Abba, Father." The same Spirit agrees with our spirit that we are God's children. But if we are children, we are also heirs. We are God's heirs and fellow heirs with Christ if we suffer with Him so that we can also be glorified with Him." Dear reader, God is not mad with you; you are not going through something difficult because He enjoys seeing you struggle. No, we live in a sinful world, and sometimes bad things happen to good people, and occasionally bad people seem to get away its murder.

Yes, He cares about your situation, and as we learn to seek Him, to draw closer to Him, He promises to provide for us. He truly wants to make sure we make it to the end, and we make it to eternity with Him, not the other place. Think of Phoenix, Arizona, just way hotter! (You have to live there for a summer to understand!) The apostle Peter who suffered greatly in his walk with God, says it best in his letter, 1 Peter 4:12-16 CEB: "Dear friends, don't be surprised about the fiery trials that have come among you to test you. These are not strange happenings. Instead, rejoice as you share Christ's suffering. You share His suffering now so that you may also have overwhelming joy when His glory is revealed. If you are mocked because of Christ's name, you are blessed, for the spirit of glory—indeed, the Spirit of

God—rests on you. Now, none of you should suffer as a murderer or thief or evildoer or rebel. But don't be ashamed if you suffer as one who belongs to Christ. Rather, honor God as you bear Christ's name. Give honor to God."

As you know by now, I've been going through what I consider a challenging wilderness experience. Many things I have lost along the way, including my ministry of 14 years. Primarily because of my poor choices, but it has also been aggravated by the additional misguided choices of others against me. Yet, I do have faith that even though I may suffer, or have pain, even as I am rejected, pushed aside, just like with Jesus, I rejoice because I believe God is ultimately in control. Even if I can't see it yet, I believe it. Tell me, do you see the air you breathe? No, yet you don't question whether it is there or not; you just accept that it is there, and you breathe in and out. As a matter of fact, we take over 23,000 breaths each day, over 8.4 million breaths a year. Do you doubt that air is there that many times? Not even once, right. So have faith in God to see you through whatever you are going through. He brings a breath of life and hope into our situations every second of every day; all we have to do is just believe and take it all in!

The best way I find about doing this is to stay close to His Word, and pray, and trust that He will use your situation for good, that He is preparing you for something ahead. Rejoice in that! After all, the Apostle Peter again said it best in 1 Peter 5:10 (CEB): "After you have suffered for a little while, the God of all grace, the one who called you into His eternal glory in Christ Jesus, will Himself restore, empower, strengthen, and establish you." A time of trials, a wilderness experience, a season of depression, call it what you will, it's a time where God is asking you to trust in Him even more because He loves you so much, that He wants to do what He can to make the better version of you possible. All you have to do is get on board, surrender to His will and allow Him to lead you, trust Him like you trust the air you breathe; God will always bless you in the end. It's not going to be easy at times, but it will be worth it. It's like those people that stand in lines for days to get their hands on a good bargain. We may need to wait for a bit for our release, but the eternal rewards for our faithful perseverance will always be worth it!

God truly has a high opinion of us, yet why do we still doubt His grace? Is it that we just can't see ourselves worthy of His love, of His mercy, of His kindness? While that may be true, it does not negate the fact that God still wants to love us; He still wants to be in a personal relationship with us. He still very much has predestined His creation to make a Righteous choice to follow the example of His Son. The option is always ours, regardless of what others may say, or how we may be treated, or what difficulties we may be called to journey through, God's good purpose for His children remains. The faster we learn to trust in Him, to draw ever so close to His will, the quicker we will understand the reason for our suffering, the purpose for our wilderness experience.

When God calls us, He will always prepare us, and He will always give us the tools we need. There was a wonderful message from God to Moses when He had rescued His people from slavery. God gives them all of the instructions for building the tabernacle and establishing the Jewish nation as the example of what God expected of His creation. As God gives Him the elaborate instructions on how to build this and that at the end of Exodus 31, God tells Moses that He had already called, appointed, and equipped the people necessary to accomplish all that He had commanded. Jesus does the same beautiful work of grace in each of our lives with the help of the Holy Spirit, as He trains us through life experiences, through the example of others in Scripture, and our intentional relationship with Him. He wants us to focus on others, develop their strengths and minimize their weaknesses. He desires that we follow His procedures (Scriptural Promises) to learn by example while keeping each other accountable.

God grants us a plan by which He means to give us freedom to fail but encouragement to try again. And finally, He expects a godly product from us, an outcome of spiritual fruit with the sole purpose of glorifying Him and blessing those around us. So do not be afraid to walk the road you are currently in; God will see you through it if you just submit to His will and trust in His purpose. Without a doubt, resign yourself to His perfect timing; this is the only proper choice we have. The more we fight our situation, the more it hurts, the more we try to get ourselves out of it, the more we fail. There is a reason in our pain, just like there was a significant reason in the suffering of Jesus. Even in our failures and willful disobedience, God is still working; He is still waiting for us to come to our senses, for us to realize how much He loves us and for us to live our lives for Him ultimately. In one of the darkest hours I experienced in my spiritual wilderness; I remember being up in the middle of the night and kneeling at the foot of my bed and just crying to THE LORD, asking for wisdom, asking for peace, even asking Him to get me out of my pain. I was at what I considered my end and at the point of emptiness when all I had was the remnant of my hope in Jesus. Like Job, I proclaimed, "for I awaited good, but evil came, I expected light, but gloom came." (Job 30:26 CEB). Then, I felt God reach out to me and refocus me out of my hurting condition ack to His merciful love.

Slowly, during the days and weeks that followed, God began to rebuild me, to strengthen me, to show me how much He truly loved me. Many things He has restored since, and even more than I could imagine. He has continued to bless my family and me, He has continued to walk by my side, and even when I still mess up, I have felt His tender voice calling me to stay the course. It has not been easy, and still, from time to time, I do feel a test on my faith, a needed spiritual adjustment, a little more dross removal from the purification process He began on that night. I have learned that the more I rely on Him, the better my life gets. Even though I may still suffer from time to time in this sinful world, I will hope never to doubt the good purpose of God for my life again. God keeps His promises He always does, and in fact, the resurrection or the end of Jesus' wilderness journey is a beautiful affirmation of the promises of God.

He is not on the cross, His garments were left behind in the tomb, and the tomb itself was empty! Yes, the cross is empty, and this is a promise kept! We want it to be empty because it reflects that Jesus died as a man but eventually resurrected as the Divine Son of God, making it possible for humanity to be once again reunited with our Maker. The other thing that the disciples found when they ran to the tomb to verify that Jesus was gone was His empty clothes. I knew it, yes He came back from the dead, but He got out of town as fast as He could. He totally abandoned us; they must have thought. Yet even the empty garments you see are that promised kept and serve a great purpose. The garments are a physical thing, and as Jesus travels through His own valley of shadow and death, He enters the spiritual realm where a simple burial robe served no purpose.

In the same way that Jesus had emptied Himself of His Divinity and come down to earth and surrender to death on the cross, now, He was shedding part of His physical existence and reclaiming His full Divinity as a necessary act to complete His work of restitution and reconciliation for all humanity through all of time. He who would ascend back to Heaven had descended to earth to live amongst us, to preach good news to us, and ultimately to show us the ways we must go. In shedding His clothing, Jesus reminds us, mere humans, that our existence is not just an earthly one, but one meant for a spiritual realm where we may not be wearing clothing as we experience them here on earth. The empty garments say to me that He was once again fully Divine. Yes, as the second person of the trinity, Jesus exists in the flesh, but I do not believe it is an earthly body, but rather the heavenly one that we will all receive one day for our faithful service. No, He did not break His promise and abandoned us, but instead, He came back, once again now in a heavenly form. It looked like a human body to those who saw Him, but it was indeed a heavenly host!

We know this from the promise He made to the man crucified by Him, he who sought forgiveness from Christ. Jesus told him, today, you will be with me in Paradise. Meaning when Jesus Himself died, He went straight to the presence of God, while His earthly body remains in the cave. Eventually, Jesus was restored for our benefit so that we could experience His kept promises. I had the privilege a few years back to visit the location that is believed to have been the room where Jesus was buried. Whether it is the actual place or not, I must confess there was a feeling of awe and hope when I entered that cave. And as I saw the empty room, it did not make me feel sad, but in fact, it brought great hope to my life at that very moment.

The cross was empty, the garments were empty, and the tomb itself was empty to their surprise. If you remember the events around the resurrection of Jesus, we are told that an Angel had rolled the stone away from the tomb entrance. This was not done so that Jesus could get out. No, remember He has Himself a brand new heavenly body, including the ability to phase through matter as we understand it. No, the Angel rolls the stone back so that His disciples could see the empty tomb. The empty tomb is not a broken promise, Jesus has not abandoned us, but it is an excellent testimony that He had indeed kept His word. He was not dead but was genuinely alive, and for a short time, He appears to be doing just that, transitioning between this earthly body into a heavenly one.

You see, we do not need to hope to see Jesus to have a conversation of great inspiration with us. We do not need to wish he would come and be by our side in our darkest of days. He is here; He is with you; through His Holy Spirit, He already lives in you, if you have surrender yourself to Him if you have come to trust in Him. When you read the Bible, Jesus tells us, we get to know the Father, so the answers to all of our situations are already there. No need to hope to see Jesus; experience Him right now, listen for his comfort as he uses others to bring you peace, as He reaches out to you from your heart, through your mind, and in your faithful actions. One day as I had just about lost all the hope I had left and allowed myself to think that perhaps death was the only release due to the intense pain I was going through caused by my separation and previous poor choices, God sent an angel with a message of hope.

As I had cried to Heavens during the previous days, wondering why God had abandoned me, I was at work working as a cashier when this little old lady came through my line with an adult child who clearly had some developmental issues. This young man was loud and disruptive, and I thought to myself, oh no, why are they coming through my lane? I tried my best to focus on the lady, but all noticed her child's behaviors. I tried to pay him no attention, yet as I was bagging the groceries, I noticed he was standing by the bag area staring at me, so I looked his way and said, hi, to which he responded, "Moy, God wanted me to tell you that He loves you and not to worry about a thing for He will take care of you." And just like that, he went back to his old childish behavior. To this day, I will never forget the incredible sense of hope and joy that filled every inch of my body as I tried all that I could not to break down in tears on the spot. Yet he was right; in my time of deep depression, God was reaching out to me through a complete stranger to bring me hope.

Be mindful as to whose voice you are listening to. God is seeking to comfort us through our experiences, through strangers, through His Holy Spirit. Jesus could have listened to the enemy's temptation, to the doubt in His own heart, to the refusal of His inner circle, yet He chooses to keep listening to the Father's guidance, seeking His counsel! The Psalm writer warns us of such a failure when in Psalm 1, he contrasts the righteous person and the wicked one. The wicked one goes down the wrong path. Listening to the wrong people, refusing to accept the truths right in front of his face, surrounding himself with negative people, and slowing those negative voices begins to influence him.

On the contrary, the righteous person who chooses to remain near God will enjoy a firm foundation, be fed by a gracious Father, produce spiritual outcomes that will bless others around him. He will also secure the assurance of God to carry on and discover what godly success is all about. All by remaining near to the source of life, seeking Him in the Word of the living God, and practicing His mercy and grace in others. There is a great Christian chorus from Craig Musseau, whose words have served to help me stand firm even in the midst of the most challenging times. Words that remind me of the goodness of God, I pray they may bring you to hope right now. Remember, there may be times when our wilderness experiences will seem preordained, yet they are always meant for our growth and development. Trust in God's plan and rejoice in His Love for what He will do in you and through you. Seek His will and rely on His strength to get you through it. Be reminded of the faithful song by Craig Mussea, "Good to me:"

"I cry out for your hand of mercy to heal me. I am weak, I need your love to free me. Oh LORD, my Rock, my strength in weakness. Come rescue me, oh LORD. You are my hope, your promise never fails me, and my desire is to follow You forever."

God is not a God of disorder but peace (1 Corinthians 14:33 CEB); therefore, even during our trials and temptations, during our deepest wilderness experiences, let us be at ease, knowing that He will bring order to our disorder if we trust His purpose. Never stop working at what God calls you to do, even if it's to walk right into a wilderness experience. Ensure that your actions bless others and bring value to their lives and your Christian Faith. That night after the experience with that young man, my life and perception of my situation began to change from despair to hope. Seek to understand God's purpose in your pain and then share in His clear vision and mission for you. Always keep a big picture mentality seeing a few steps in front of you. By all means, please keep order and common sense alive. After all, it is the example of an orderly God in which we trust! To God be all the glory, He who allows difficulty in our lives, but only because He knows it will prepare us to enjoy the future blessings He has in store for us. Come with me, Holy Spirit, as I continue to walk close to you, as I cry to you for mercy, grant it, let me find hope in the fulfillment of your promises. Help me to keep my eyes upon you and live for you every day, no matter what road I am called to travel.

Questions to keep exploring.

How can learning to live in God's providence help us make it through our wilderness experience?

Do we feel a sense of urgency or a call to godly action due to our journey through the valleys of darkness and death?

Are you able to identify the potential that God sees in you in spite of the shortcomings you see in yourself?

How is your spiritual strength doing now, when compared to the beginning of your tribulations?

What are you doing to prepare your testimony as a result of this time of testing, to reflect your newfound spiritual maturity?

What are you willing to give up in your life so that the will of God may be fulfilled in you and others around you?

What lessons of hope, faith, and trust are you holding on to from your trials and tribulations? How are you applying those lessons in your life to help you grow closer to God?

10

PETER AND THE BOYS

Wilderness Experiences Brought Upon
by Immaturity and Disbelief.

"Then all the disciples left Jesus and ran away."
Matthew 26:56 (CEB)

When we focus on the storm rather than on the Savior, we will always sink! This is a reality that not only Peter experienced when he faithfully stepped out of the boat in the middle of an actual storm, but something all of the disciples would experience on the night that Jesus was finally arrested as they all ran away to save their lives. But why did they run? Why surrender to their fears so quickly? For as long as I can remember, the disciples have always been portrayed as older bearded men who followed Jesus around like some sort of positive influencing goon squad, bringing hope to the masses. Yet, the more I think about how they behaved and how they reacted, the less I think of them as mature men and more as hormonally imbalanced teens! Hear me out!

Grown-up men usually don't get themselves in trouble with what they say, and they tend to be more tactical when they speak, unlike Peter often did. On the other hand, young men full of passion and impatience are well known for shooting their mouths off and living life for their emotions. Suppose I look at the disciples as adolescents. In that case, it begins to paint a clearer picture and even answer why Peter jumped to action when Jesus was being arrested, and why eventually they all took off as fast as their young legs would carry them. They probably were the type of boys that did not excel in school and ended up going back to work in their family trades rather than continuing the study of God's Word. Eventually, when a Rabbi, a teacher, calls them to follow Him, they literally walk away from their livelihoods to learn from Him. I don't think responsible adults would make such a drastic move. Reminds me of how I previously acted and the frustrations I caused so many. So what do we know about these young men?

Jesus first called the brothers Peter and Andrew to follow him. Probably were the eldest in the group. They had served as disciples of Jesus' cousin, John the Baptizer, where they undoubtedly learned about the coming Messiah. (John 1:40-42 CEB). Peter is the only one we know was actually married. He came across as the spokesperson for the group and was eventually tasked with taking the good news of Jesus to the Jews (Galatians 2:7 CEB). Catholic tradition tells us that when Peter was a martyr for his faith, that he asked to be hung upside down on the cross, as he did not feel worthy to die in the same manner that his LORD had been killed. On the other hand, Andrew will always be remembered as the one who brought Peter to Jesus. A great service, to say the least. He would be the first to follow Jesus after John referred to Him as the lamb of God (John 1:36 CEB). Church history also tells us that Andrew was known as a passionate preacher and made great contributions to the early church.

The next two were also brothers, the sons of thunder were James and John. They appear to have been fishing partners of Peter and Andrew and probably knew each other for some time. James was trusted by Jesus, as he was part of the inner circle of three that were often with Jesus when great events were taking place (Mark 5:37, 14:33, and Matthew 17:1 CEB). James was the first disciple to be martyred for the faith and recorded in Scripture (Acts 12:1-3 CEB). His brother John was known as the disciple that Jesus loved (John 3:23 CEB) and the one that goes on to write the Gospel according to John; 1st, 2nd, and 3rd Epistles of John plus the final Revelations of God to His creation. John's Gospel takes a different approach to the other three so-called synoptic Gospels (Matthew, Mark, and Luke). Instead of focusing on what Jesus said or did, John shows us who Jesus was, an account focused on the identity of Christ. After his exile to the island of Patmos, eventually, he is allowed to return to Ephesus, where he governs over the church there and in nearby Asia.

Jesus next called Phillip, and we do not know much about him. Phillip was actually his Greek name. He was known as a passionate evangelist who introduces Nathanael to the one Moses had foretold (Jesus). He is believed to have been martyred in Hierapolis, Greece. Nathanael next was from Galilee and was recognized by Jesus Himself as a true Israelites in whom there was no deceit (John 1:47 CEB). It is believed that he carried the Gospel to India yet was ultimately crucified and beheaded in Armenia. Matthew would come next on the list. He was the worse of the worse to be chosen so far. A Jewish Tax-collector who worked for the Roman government and more than likely stole from the people to pay the Romans and pack his own pockets. Matthew, of course, eventually writes a very detailed account of Jesus' life, a book directed at the Jewish community to connect their faith in the books of the law and bring them into the fulfillment of God's covenant through Jesus. Towards the end of his life, he is credited with bringing the Gospel to Egypt and further south into Ethiopia.

Number eight is Thomas, or as we know him best, doubting Thomas. He was a well-known skeptic who often spoke his mind. In John 11:16 (CEB), we account for his brashness when after the death of Lazarus, he suggests to the crew that they too should go with Jesus to Bethany and be willing to die with Him. Church tradition strongly suggests that he also took the Gospel into India, where he was ironically killed with a spear. Number nine is James the Less, of whom we know not much at all, except that Jesus chose him as a disciple. Therefore, we know he was trained and empowered to be a messenger of the Gospel of Salvation. Nothing to shy away from! Number ten brings us to Simon, the Zealot of whom we know very little as well. Tradition tells us he took the Gospel to West Africa and eventually ended up north on the island we call Great Britain today. Second, to last, we have Judah, no not that one, the other Judah, who seemed concerned with who Jesus would reveal Himself to (John 14:22 CEB). Church tradition tells us he took the Gospel to Modern day Turkey and eventually was clubbed to death.

Last and certainly the least is a name we would all recognize Judas Iscariot; yes, this is the one you were thinking about before. He was outspoken for the wrong reasons. He was greedy and misguided. He is the one Jesus spoke off when he said, "did I Myself not choose you, the twelve, and yet one of you is a devil? ...one of the twelve was going to betray me." (John 6:70-71 CEB). He received the same training as the other eleven and spent the same amount of time with the Master as the others, yet he chose his own pitiful path. Of course, this is the traitor, the one who betrayed Jesus for a measly 30 silver coins. His regret was so great that he found himself with no other potential options but to take his own life in quite a graphic manner. (Acts 1:18-19 CEB) He felt such remorse and had no other way to express it that he hung himself. (Matthew 27:3-5 CEB). Unlike Peter, who struggled with his own denial, Judas of Iscariot could not come to a place of repentance, and so death seemed like his only release from the pain he felt after selling out an innocent man.

In my own wilderness experience, I had asked myself why did I give into my fear, why did I at times betray my LORD when things looked a bit grim? You see, I am ashamed to confess that when things were really up in the air, and there was no perceived hope in sight, I too ran. I mean, I got in a moving truck and moved from one coast to the other. Over two thousand miles between me and my troubles. I thought I could outrun them, which I couldn't. I thought I could outrun God, which I also didn't. All I was left with was the guilt for my reactive behavior when I threw it all away. It wasn't until I confessed my actionable failures to God and until I accepted my wrongdoing that THE LORD liberated me from my guilt. I was able to become receptive and better conductive of His grace in my life, once again. It wasn't an easy step. Plenty of spiritually dark nights, filled with tears and sorrow, were like Judah's Iscariot; even ending it all seemed like a preferable solution to the pain I felt. Yet, thank God that even though He allowed me to walk on the edge of the abyss of death, He was there to yank me back into His merciful arms and His safety through the help of a good friend.

The prophet Samuel speaking of God, said, "You are the one who saves people who suffer, but your eyes are against the proud. You bring them down! You are my lamp, LORD; THE LORD illumines my darkness. I can charge into battle; with my God, I can leap over a wall. God! His way is perfect; THE LORD's Word is tried and true. He is a shield for all who take refuge in Him." 2 Samuel 22:28-31 (CEB). What helped me begin my journey out of my wilderness experience, much like Peter's case, was a contrite heart, followed by repentance. On top of that, the belief that God was still my refuge, that He must still have a plan for me, that He intended to light my way again. That thought gave me enough hope to make it through each day, a hope that was multiplied in my heart, one that continues to grow in me with every passing day.

I have come to experience a closer connection to the source, my supplier of hope, the Holy Spirit, because I once again realized what it meant that He is alive in me! (1 John 4:4 CEB). Repentance also allowed me to forgive myself, and it was that forgiveness that caused my emotional and spiritual wounds to begin to heal. You see, if all we do is run and dig ourselves deeper into our guilt, then we leave no room for God's grace. Therefore, we must learn even in the darkest hour of our souls to simply shake off the world, our enemies, even the temptations of the devil and get up and get moving forward in life, in the strength of THE LORD.

There is a great story of a farmer who had his mule fall into a hole and couldn't afford to pay to get it out. He decided that the only option was to bury the animal alive in the hole. He began to shovel in the dirt, and as each shovel full of dirt hit the mule's back, it simply shook it off, and it fell to its side. As the farmer continued to shovel dirt in, the mule just kept shaking each portion off and slowly began to rise as it stood on the dirt falling around her, until finally, the hole had risen enough that the animal could simply walk out of its would-be grave. The truth is that the experiences of life will sometimes overpower us, intended as they may have been to destroy us, to bury us alive, yet we must never give in or give up, but persevere, shake it off and rise!

As the disciples ran away, their wilderness experience was about to begin. Even Peter and John, who watched from afar, witness their LORD being beaten and eventually crucified to death. How could this be? They had put all of their hope on this Messiah, Yeshua Ha-Mashiach, Jesus the Christ, and now He was dead. Even worse, how could they forget all that Jesus had told them? So much so that when Jesus does return from the dead, He finds some of them back at their previous professions, just gone back to doing what was familiar to them. This group of young men were about to learn the reality that when we only follow Jesus or hang on to our faith only when things are going well, it's never enough. We must also seek the strength necessary to remain close to our Father, to live in His hope even when things don't go as planned. Trust me, this is a lesson I have been practicing for a very long time; after all, I am a Miami Dolphins football team fan!!! Things never go as I hope with those guys!

A lesson that even Peter eventually learned, when he reminded his audience in 1 Peter 1:3 (CEB), to "bless the name of our Saviors, on account of His vast mercy, He has given us new birth. We, he says, have been born anew into a living hope through the resurrection of Jesus Christ from the dead." We know that Peter wept bitterly when Jesus' predicted that he would deny Him three times. Peter was so sure that he would remain faithful, yet when he saw that he was incapable of taking on the same cross he swore he could carry just days before, it cut him deep to his heart to find out that he truly could not. I can only imagine that the next few days were truly heartbreaking for Peter and the others. No wonder when Jesus meets Peter by the lake, He gets Peter to proclaim his allegiance and love on three occasions. Three times Peter denied Jesus, and now three times, Jesus reassures his calling and is reinstates him back into faithful action. (John 21:15-25 CEB)

Is it possible for anyone to fall from grace into a time of wilderness? Even King Saul, God's anointed, he who prophesied, was full of the Spirit, brought a kingdom together, organized an army, and defeated his enemies time after time, had a very interesting turn of events in his life, when he took his eyes off God and dared to think that he knew better than God. I use to think I was invulnerable, greater than my teachers, more important than my supervisors. Yet, part of my own story was my pride and my inability to simply stop and let my actions match my faith.

After I ran, I use to think that maybe God was done with me, that He had indeed cast me away. That erroneous thought process led me down some dark thought patterns that still scare me to this day. But God is faithful, my friends, and He promises never to leave us nor forsake us. So we must fight against those selfish tendencies and trust in God's ultimate plan. When we can align our thoughts, speech, and conduct with God's purpose and make them consistent with our prayer requests, we will receive the answer from God. Even if it means waiting for the answer to manifest, we must wait patiently, and we will have our answer because God loves His children, and He is always ready to provide for their needs. (Matthew 7:11 CEB). Don't get tired of asking; pray without ceasing, (1 Thessalonians 5:17 CEB). Hallelujah! Be an overcomer of your situation. Bring everything indeed to God in prayer!

Sometimes the wilderness experience is the only way we will change or abandon a destructive behavior. During this process, my wife reminded me how even after the worst forest fires, the ground is healthier for it, and new growth can come about. From destruction comes newness. God used a similar example with the prophet Jeremiah when He had him visit the potters home, and he saw first hand how God would shape us and, when necessary, can break us down and begin again with the same clay. (Jeremiah 18:1-11 CEB). Dear reader, tomorrow is the hope we long for, yesterday is the lesson we have learned and today is where we put it all into practice. Meaning the experiences and the hope. Gold itself rarely exists in its pure form, but it is usually mixed in with other metals and minerals. A great amount of heat must be applied to separate what is valuable and what is not. God is doing this very thing in us. Allowing the heat of our situation to melt away the impurities, the dross if you will, and then He must chisel those useless bits away. This will be a painful experience, I know, but one that will increase our value to its full potential.

Once again, Peter speaking from his early life experience in 1 Peter 5:6 (CEB) reminds us: to humble ourselves under God's power so that He may raise us up in the last day. Throw all our anxiety onto Him because He cares about us. Be clearheaded. Keep alert as the accuser, the devil, is on the prowl like a roaring lion, seeking someone to devour. Resist him, standing firm in the faith. Do so in the knowledge that our fellow believers are enduring the same suffering throughout the world. After you have suffered for a little while, the God of all grace, the one who called you into His eternal glory in Christ Jesus, will Himself restore, empower, strengthen, and establish you." (1 Peter 5:6-10 CEB). As we saw from the introduction of these young apostles, this is exactly what God did for these boys, that is, those who repented from their actions and returned to Him.

How many of us have ever made or plan to make some sort of New Year's Resolutions? Don't be shy; I know many of us have or will make them. They range from losing weight to spending more time with family, getting a better job, and reading the entire Bible or more. There are many different resolutions that we want to accomplish during the new beginnings of a new year! But have you ever wondered why we do this? I believe that it is because along with the new year comes new hope, a fresh start, and the choice to keep moving forward and not dwelling in the past – to not dwell on the things that were not previously accomplished. We have the choice to look to the future, and more importantly, we have an opportunity to see what God can accomplish through us in the year. From past experiences, most of us know that resolutions don't often work well because we have to depend on ourselves, and when we depend on ourselves, we often fail. We don't reach our goals or resolutions; we let ourselves down, give up, and even get discouraged.

Wanting to come out of our wilderness journey is a good thing to hope for and, I feel it should be treated differently than other situations in our lives. What should be different is our approach to the potential growth it will bring. The Apostle Paul speaks of this to the church in Phillipi when he wrote to them: "Do nothing out of selfish ambition or vain conceit, but in humility consider others better than yourselves. Your attitude should be the same as that of Christ Jesus: Who, being in very nature God, did not consider equality with God something to be grasped, but made

Himself nothing, taking the very nature of a servant, being made in human likeness." (Philippians 2:1-11 CEB). What then, if our resolution for any new year would be to be more like Jesus? Right away, you might think, "Ahhh, Moy, that's a really hard resolution; how in the world are we going to keep this one? Well, let me tell you that it is very possible. When we seek to be more like Christ, we focus less on ourselves and more on others. I believe this behavior will certainly help us come out of our spiritual desert into a flowing life of hope.

In attempting to be more like Jesus, we cannot insist that we can accomplish such a great thing all on our own, but we must realize once and for all that we need God's help. His help through His love and grace, which we can receive by asking Him in prayer for such a transformation in our lives. Through the teachings and examples, we have from Jesus Christ in studying the Bible and being transformed by the renewing of our minds. To off course in the leading and guiding of the Holy Spirit in our lives, especially as we walk through the valley of the shadow of death. It can happen for you! Paul again proclaims, in Ephesians 4:22-24 (CEB), "You were taught, with regard to your former way of life, to put off your old self, which is being corrupted by its deceitful desires; to be made new in the attitude of your minds; and to put on the new self, created to be like God in true righteousness and holiness."

You see, with God's grace, we have the opportunity to be reborn and have a fresh start in life through the life and death of His Son Jesus Christ. The disciples experienced this very truth. Jesus gave us all the options, the very real choice of choosing to leave it all behind and choosing to change the pessimistic attitudes of our lives and start a new one. The young passionate disciples did, so can we! Because God loves us so much, He will grant us every effort needed to be more like His Son. He offers His ear to us in prayer, He listens to our requests, and if it is in His will, if He feels it will benefit our spiritual development, God will grant it. He knows the desires of our hearts and can see our intentions, and if we truly desire to be like Jesus – He will bless us with that gift. Peter and the boys had spent all that time listening to Jesus, now all of His lessons are ringing in their heads, and as soon as Jesus returns from the dead, it is as if they began to be activated. The sorrow was replaced with joy, their sense of loss was taken over by hope, and their loneliness was fulfilled by God's great purpose and direction and eventually by the promised Counselor that would take Jesus' place!

Our Heavenly Father does not want us to remain in darkness, but He has many good gifts waiting for us, for those who ask Him! (Matthew 7:11 CEB). God in heaven, our Father, who knows what we need, will give to us when we earnestly ask Him the attitude and perception of Christ. To be like Jesus simply means that we will follow the example of Christ Himself in our lives, something the Disciples finally did. 1 Peter 2:21-24 (CEB) we read: "To this you were called, because Christ suffered for you, leaving you an example that you should follow in His steps. He committed no sin, and no deceit was found in His mouth. When they hurled their insults at Him, He did not retaliate; when He suffered, He made no threats. Instead, He entrusted Himself to Him, who judges justly. He Himself bore our sins in His body on the tree, so that we might die to sin in our lives and live for righteousness; by His wounds, WE have been healed." Yes, finally they got it, and so can we!

Like the disciples who ultimately learned the meaning of trusting in Jesus, we too must learn to entrust our lives to God. No matter who ridicules us, or who controls us, or who insults and abuses us, do so knowing that God will remain in control of it all. He always believes that He can bring good from every negative situation we may encounter. You see, God not only sent His Son to die for us and grant the only way to have everlasting, eternal life but also that He may live in this world as a man to suffer; to be tempted, to be human and know how it is to live in a world constantly being tempted by evil. Trust me, Jesus understands our situation, our condition, and He came to the earth in human form not immune to the elements of this world but subject to them and yet lived a Holy life – giving us the perfect example of how we must and can indeed live by.

Now, we can only learn of how He lived by reading the Bible and studying it so that we may, in turn, mimic Christ and see the benefits of being in an attitude of prayer with God. Loving without end and complete humbleness – just to name a few as we seek to be more intentional in our approach to our living for God. Then as we draw nearer to Jesus and begin to behave as He did more and more, and as we trust in the Spirit to guide us in serving others. May we encourage each other along this walk of faith and as we recognize that we have been saved and have Christ in our hearts. We should recognize that we do have some encouragement, some influence for changing our ways and being reborn to be different from the rest of the world and start a new way of living based on our experiences with Jesus. For you see, once being united with Jesus, there should be a change just like when ordinary white daisies are placed in water that is tinted with blue food coloring; eventually, the white flowers absorb the colorful water and turn blue.

We are like those daisies taking on the same color that surrounds us, changing the way we appear to others. We are the same person but with different attributes and character. Like Christ, we must think of others first; then, we must be humble and not selfish or think of ourselves better than others. We are influenced by the one who dwells in us, and the more time we spend in prayer, the more time we spend in God's Word, the more we will be influenced to renovate our lives. Like in high school, many adolescents are influenced by those they are around the most, and they feel like they need to please those closest to them by quickly submitting to their suggestions for living. Whether it is a good or a bad influence, it will motivate them.

We must surround ourselves with good things for our spiritual lives – active prayer life, intentional studying of God's Word, and willingness to seek and listen for guidance. Not only should we resolve each new year to be more like Jesus, but we must also commit to being in deeper fellowship and freedom with the Holy Spirit. Which go hand in hand. 2 Corinthians 3:17-18 (ESV) - "Now THE LORD is the Spirit, and where the Spirit of THE LORD is, there is freedom. And we, who with unveiled faces all reflect THE LORD's glory, are being transformed in His likeness with ever-increasing glory, for this comes from THE LORD, who is the Spirit." Like the disciple, we have seen the benefits of knowing God's love for us and being united with Christ and learning through His example of living here on earth. We need to realize the daily help we will need to be transformed and renewed each day for spiritual growth and working together with others. We must remember that this all comes from THE LORD, not us but from God, who is Spirit. Meaning that we need to be in tune with our spiritual needs. I truly believe this is what we see in the eventual spiritual successes of the disciples of Jesus. And I believe it is the same work He is continually producing in my own life and yours.

When we get in touch with the Spirit in us, we find a whole new world of spiritual possibilities. We have a new perspective on everything, a fresh voice that gives us fresh insight. And we can only get to that point if we open our minds and hearts to God's Spirit, allowing a different power in our lives to rule us instead of the old one that has gotten us nowhere. Philippians 2:1 (CEB) again reminds us, "Is there fellowship together in the Spirit? Are your hearts tender and compassionate? Then make me truly happy by agreeing wholeheartedly with each other, loving one another, and working together with one mind and purpose." If we are in fellowship with the Holy Spirit, it will make our joy complete because we will be a step closer to being like-minded, having the same love, being one in Spirit and purpose. Being like Christ. Which simply means loving without end and being active in God's plan and purpose for our lives. Seeing the complete picture of what our purpose in life is according to that great plan.

As we speak of the spiritual things, of our spiritual being, and the intimate connection with the Holy Spirit and God, I can feel some of you thinking, "Wow, am I really ready for this serious commitment?" "Am I up for this next step in my life with Christ?" Just like anything in life, there are questions and concerns of the unknown, of things that we don't know too much about. It is just like when a new couple has a baby. When we first found out we were pregnant with our daughter Jocy, we had so many emotions. We were happy, scared, anxious, and even unsure if we could handle this experience. After she was born, my wife even said she understood why women are pregnant for nine months. It's not just a time for the child to develop, but also it is a time of preparation for the expectant parents. With experience comes hope. When our son Josh was born, we felt like experts!

Just like awaiting a child to be born, there are so many similarities in waiting for a new life and a fuller life with the Holy Spirit's help. It's something new and different, something that we feel we are not ready for but don't worry, it won't happen all of a sudden, but God will give you time. He will reveal His Holy Spirit in stages in a progression so that you are not overwhelmed by the greatest blessing of all. Be reassured today knowing that even though taking our spiritual lives to the next step may seem a little scary, remember that God will only give us good things and does grant us the freedom to ask for more in this relationship with Him. When you are willing and ready, He always provides. If you want to lose weight, or exercise more, or watch less tv, maybe drink less coffee, go ahead and make those commitments. Ensure you have a good support structure, accountability partner, and motivation to ensure you succeed. But you can also trust in THE LORD always and make your resolutions are those things He already desires for you, to be more like His Son Jesus, by depending more each day on His Holy Spirit.

Unlike other resolutions you may have made in the past, this one will be more likely to come to reality because we won't be doing it on our own, but we will have God's help. If God is for us, who then can be against us, right? Only we can bring ourselves up for failure by not trying, by not trusting, by not submitting entirely to God's will for our lives starting today. One of my favorite church choruses of all time reminds me as the disciples eventually learned that to be like Jesus should be our only desire. The words say, "To be like Jesus, this hope possesses me in every thought and deed; this is my aim, my creed. To be like Jesus, this hope possesses me, His Spirit helping me, like Him I'll be "Any wilderness journey we may be called to travel will ultimately always lead us to Christlikeness.

Jesus was preparing His team to live in full confidence of what He had taught them in Word and action. The leadership guru John Maxwell speaks of the law of the navigator when he says that anyone can steer the ship, but it takes a leader that can chart the course. As imitators of Jesus, like the disciples, we may be able to lead our way, but only under His leadership could we navigate His purpose for our lives. As a result, we are called to adjust our priorities and follow God's blueprint for our lives. Followed by living up to our capabilities by using our God-given abilities and strengths. Learn to draw near to Him and trust in His ultimate plan, and last but not least, live in the experience of His grace and be excited to put our faith in Him into action. Peter and the boys eventually understood this, and because they lived out these characteristics, we now have the Christian Church!

If Peter or any of the disciples were here, I am sure they would tell us that the place between what was and what can be is where we come to make a conscious choice to trust in God and live in His hope. Even when faced with opposition, especially as we feel we have the right answers and training, we must still trust God. To simply focus on our ideas to be proven right will damper our ability to be effective for the glory of God in the future. Jesus wanted his team to be future-minded, and He desires the same for us. Forget what is behind, learn from it, but leave it in the past and move forward in faith. As Jesus taught us, forgive and forget that we may grow in God's purpose for our lives.

Our Heavenly Father, as we proclaim today our desire to be like Jesus, to follow Him, to learn from His life, may we see that we all need your help to get to the next level of our Christian faith in you. As we ask you in prayer to be more like your Son, let your Spirit possess us, take over us in the way we live, in the things we do and say. That we may reflect your likeness and that all may see just how much you can transform such a sinner like me; that I may be a real hope to others. Showing us in the love you give, the joy you provide, the peace you bring to humble ourselves before you and others.

Thank You, LORD, for all you do, for the plans you have for each one of us, and the hope for this new life you grant us when we learn to trust in you in the middle of our storms when we come through our wilderness experience. Help us to live in full dependence and obedience to your Holy Spirit. Thank you, LORD, that we don't have to live in our past failures or disappointments. Instead, we will trade all of our sorrows; we will trade all of our pains for the joy of THE LORD. We'll say yes to you, to your will, to your purpose, and your guidance from now and forever. As we seek you, please let us indeed find you!

Questions to keep exploring.

How does your journey help you humble yourself before God and seek to make amends with those you hurt?

What are you doing to remove the entangled sins of your past to live differently than when the spiritual battles first began?

What intentional actions are you taking daily to commit your life to the will of God?

How is God using your past experiences to be a blessing to others?

How can suffering and sadness turn around into hope and joy in you today?

11

THE MAIN MAN SAUL OF TARSUS (PAUL)

A Wilderness Experience as a New Way of Life, Aligning Us to a Preordained Path Leading Us to Eternity with God.

"A thorn in my body, a messenger from Satan, sent to torment me so that I wouldn't be conceited. I pleaded with THE LORD three times for it to leave me alone. He said to me, "My grace is enough for you, because when I am weak, then I am stroking." 2 Corinthians 12:7-10 (CEB)

Wilderness experiences can at times be journeys through ongoing spiritual battles. Times of brokenness, persecution, and perseverance, but also, as we have seen, a time of new beginnings and hope. I believe the Apostle Paul's main wilderness experience was one of the mind, one intended to establish something great. The Church. Don't get me wrong, he certainly also had plenty of physical pains in his journey. We know that because of his actions before his encounter with Jesus, Saul persecuted and tortured many people, and perhaps the enemy of this world used those actions to torment him mentally.

There is no doubt about it, Saul the Pharisee was a bully, and I have told you, I cannot stand bullies. They are manipulative, and they abuse their positions of power from a politician to a schoolyard offender. They use their positions to elevate themselves and their minions while diminishing the existence of others for their selfish pride. Bullies terrorize, abuse, and often do it under the assumption that because they are bigger, or stronger, or more popular with the masses because they know better, or worse, they see themselves as God's supreme representative, this somehow entitles them to treat others with content and impute their authority. Because of that, I will always stand up against bullies and their injustices no matter the cost. It reminds me of the past bullies in my life who, even though I took a righteous stand against them, how they still won, how they defeated me, humiliated me, and to some degree, they are still trying to keep me down. I do, however, wait patiently for God's justice every day.

Saul hated the newly founded Jewish sect referred to as Christians or followers of Christ. He took it upon himself as a member of the Pharisees, a sect within the ruling priestly class, made up of laymen and scribes, to persecute this growing group wherever they might be and snuff them out of existence; all with the blessing of the Jewish religious leadership (The Sadducees). Be sure of the terrible things Saul had done to these Christ-followers in the name of his misguided and shortsighted view of the Jewish faith! Later on, after his conversion and as he now is working diligently to advance the very cause of Christ, now Paul pleads with God to remove a thorn on his side, as he referenced it, and God's response was, basically no, rely on my grace for you instead. It will be sufficient. For when you are weak, my strength is made complete. No immediate release, no quick right answers, no deliverance from emotional pain and frustration, just a simple, trust me. But, how do we do that in the middle of something that is unmistakably painful? Why is it that God just doesn't reveal to us the answers, that we may do what is right, make the right choices that will lead us down the path He has set for us?

Do you struggle with the thoughts of your past? Do you wish God would just reset your mind and erase it all, that you may begin with a new slate? Don't we all, but that's not usually the case. The truth is simple, and God wants us to seek Him, to depend on Him, not ourselves. The memory of our past mistakes may be just the thing that keeps us close to His grace and not running back to our depravity and sin. This is why God gave us a ten-step goodwill plan (Ten Commandments), metaphorically speaking. A road map spelling out His expectations for our interaction with Him and what we should do? Yet time after time, we choose to do our own thing and not follow His design for us. Because we do have free will, often we freely don't choose His way, even as we claim to live the life of one of His followers. Think about it, and I know deep inside you agree this is true.

Paul himself later proclaimed to the Ephesians as much: "Bless the God and Father of our LORD Jesus Christ! He has blessed us in Christ with every spiritual blessing that comes from heaven. God chose us in Christ to be Holy and blameless in God's presence before the creation of the world. God destined us to be His adopted children through Jesus Christ because of His love. This was according to His goodwill and plan and to honor His glorious grace that He has given to us freely through the Son whom He loves. We have been ransomed through His Son's blood, and we have forgiveness for our failures based on His overflowing grace, which He poured over us with wisdom and understanding. God revealed His hidden design to us according to His goodwill and the plan that He intended to accomplish through His Son. This is what God planned for the climax of all times: to bring all things together in Christ, the things in heaven along with the things on earth. We have also received an inheritance in Christ. We were destined by the plan of God, who accomplishes everything according to His design." Ephesians 1:3-11 (CEB)

Like Paul, we must not seek righteousness by mere obedience to the law. Instead of a coffee table faith that it's only on display or a Sunday school faith that is minimalist in action and pious in nature, or even a knowledge-based faith that only lives out its intentions in our heads. Instead, we must remember that faith is a verb and must be put into action, a faith that lives and breaths every day, trusting in the hope that Jesus has brought into our own lives and turn around and show the same hope, peace, and love to others. As we close our journey on the wilderness experience, I challenge us to think of this question: does God require my brokenness in order that I may lay down my pride and be all I can be in his eyes? After all, a contrite and repentant heart is all He wants from us. A broken spirit is our sacrifice! (Psalm 51:17 CEB) No need anymore for a fancy drawn-out animal sacrifice, just a heart that seeks His heart, a heart that longs for God's compassion, willing to be set apart from this world that we may better serve God and the needs of His creation.

Paul proclaims that God's grace is sufficient in the middle of his own battles! Sometimes the wilderness is where we reside, perhaps so that we may help others who lead themselves there to find their way out. Ongoing feelings of insufficiency or falling short or not feeling as one should, content and happy, can blur our understanding of God's grace and prevent us from transitioning from our brokenness to hopefulness, reflecting a Godly character in the way we live our lives. As in the events of David and Mephibosheth, who was the only surviving Son of his friend Jonathan, the last surviving family member of crazy King Saul. (2 Samuel 9) We come before the King and deserve death, our sin cripples us, yet God shows us kindness, does not give us what we had coming but invites us to His table. The King restores us. Even if later on we betray him again.

Life doesn't always work out as we planned, yet that doesn't stop God from fulfilling His will in us. You see, aside from all that Paul suffered, whether physically or emotionally, Paul carries on with the purpose for the Church that Christ continually establishes through our obedient faith in action. A church that was established and continues through the suffering we have identified of many of His faithful servants, including perhaps you and me as well. In this particular chapter in Paul's life, we come to the moment where he addresses the Christian Church in Ephesus, his home base of operations and evangelism if you will, and he does it to help them understand God's plan for them as part of His Church. Not the Church as merely a building but all those who have put their faith in Jesus for all of time.

The City of Ephesus was a central place in Asia. One of the most important cities of that day. Major trade route intercepted there. I had the blessed experience of visiting the ruins of the City a few years back, currently located in the country of Turkey, and it was awe-inspiring, to say the least, to be able to walk in the footsteps of such a giant of our faith. His letter to the Ephesians is the first letter in what is knows as the Prison Epistles. Meaning Paul wrote them from prison. Yup, you think your wilderness journey is difficult, try spending some time in jail! (I believe some of you have). Yet even knowing that this particular letter is Paul's most encouraging and optimistic letter to the Church that Christ had come to earth to establish. In short, this letter of his is also addressed to us, the members of this worldwide body of believers who are a part of the greater Universal Christian Church. From Paul, we learn that our circumstances do not need to stop us from being a blessing in the lives of others. God's grace must always be enough for us too.

In his letter, Paul describes the advantages that a believer has whose faith is in Jesus Christ, even while suffering for His Church. According to the Apostle Matthew, there is a powerful but clear message that we find in the Gospel that speaks to us clearly concerning the subject of the Church. It is a commanding statement that follows a powerful confession of faith on the part of Peter the disciple. Jesus had asked His disciples who they thought He was, and Peter answers by saying, "you are the Christ, the Son of the living God." To which Jesus replies to Peter, "on this rock I will build my church and not even the gates of the underworld will be able to stand against it." (Matthew 16:13-18 CEB) The truth of the matter is that Christ indeed came to establish a fellowship of believers, those who, through faithful obedience, would carry His work and purpose of salvation throughout the world. To live out God's original Ten Commandments in a condensed manner of simply loving God and loving our neighbor. As a result, each of us has received a special calling from God, a calling out of this world for a spiritual and heavenly purpose to be a part of the body of Christ, something that throughout the New Testament is frequently referred to as the Church. This, of course, is reflected in the life and events of Paul's wilderness journey.

Indeed the apostle Peter understood this calling as well, and he reminds us about it in 1 Peter 2:9 (CEB), where he says, "but you are a chosen race, a royal priesthood, a Holy nation, a people who are God's possession, that you may proclaim the praises of Him who called you." Our calling as part of God's Church is to serve God in the purposes of His Church. As members of the Church of Christ, we are all knit together by a supernatural kinship. Our service is a continuation of Christ's work by the inspiration of the indwelling Holy Spirit that lives in us as believers. So that in the end, we may be presented to Him - our Groom - as a perfect bride, united as one congregation before the throne of God. (2 Corinthians 11:2 CEB) It is our LORD that brings us and keeps us in fellowship with Himself and His Word. In Isaiah 59:21 (CEB), we read about God's covenant: "My Spirit who is upon you, and My words which I have placed in your mouth, won't depart from your mouth, nor from the mouth of your descendants, says THE LORD, from this time and forevermore."

The experience of being a part of Christ's Church is a revelation of God's gracious heart. The Father chose His Son so that He would take upon Himself our sins. Then He called His people (you and me) to Him, and in time we were grafted and made a part of the family of God. (Romans 11:17-23 CEB) The word church comes from the Greek word ekklesia, and as used in the Scriptures, it points to any assembly, even referring to a group of believers, and isn't that what we are a part of when we accept the sacrifice of love of Jesus on the Cross? In the book of Ephesians, we see that Paul was writing to the Church there, meaning the body of believers. As we can clearly see, the Church is not merely an institution, a specific religion, or a society or culture. It is about community and building supporting fellowship. It is imperative then that we do not allow things such as denominational preferences from leading us at any point to sacrifice our ecclesiastical mandates of service and community for the sake of uniqueness or identity that we fail to carry the simple mission of bringing hope to a people in need, no matter what suffering it may cause us.

Paul can prove he suffered sufficiently for the cause of Jesus while never compromising his faith. Aside from this thorn on his side, he surely experienced his share of troubles. "I repeat, no one should take me for a fool. But if you do, then allow me to be a fool so that I can brag like a fool for a bit." In 2 Corinthians 11:16-31 (CEB), we read his recollection of his wilderness experiences. "Are they Hebrews? So am I. Are they Israelites? So am I. Are they descendants of Abraham? (He was a Benjamite) So am I. Are they ministers of Christ? I'm speaking like a crazy person. What I've done goes well beyond what they've done. I've worked much harder. I've been imprisoned much more often. I've been beaten more times than I can count. I've faced death many times. I received the forty lashes minus one from the Jews five times. (These are the same lashes Jesus received but he way) I was beaten with rods three times. I was stoned once. I was shipwrecked three times. I spent a day and a night on the open sea. I've been on many journeys. I faced dangers from rivers, robbers, my people, and Gentiles. I faced dangers in the City, in the desert, on the sea, and from false brothers and sisters.

I faced these dangers with hard work and heavy labor, many sleepless nights, hunger and thirst, often without food, and in the cold without enough clothes. Besides all the other things I could mention, there's my daily stress because I'm concerned about all the churches. Who is weak without me being weak? Who is led astray without me being furious about it? If it's necessary to brag, I'll brag about my weaknesses. The God and Father of THE LORD Jesus, the one who is blessed forever, knows that I'm not lying." Quiet the list of suffering, yet think about all he accomplished through it, think about how all of it took place, of course, so that the Church that Jesus died to establish could be set in place and release to serve the world in need. Through the struggles of Paul, the life of faith and hope in Christ would be forever engraved in the pages of Scripture to encourage you and me and all other believers that have come before us to keep going, regardless of our journey that we may trust in God's ultimate plan of hope! How then do you think God wants to utilize your wilderness experience to advance the work of His Church?

As Paul is dealing with his own struggles, he finds it necessary to encourage others to believe! Perhaps what you may be going through, God can use to encourage others, if you allow Him. I have lost so much in my journey, and God has so graciously returned so much as well, that I feel I have no choice but to use my life's story, so far, to pen these words down and hopefully encourage you the reader, not to give up, but to keep moving forward trusting in God's perfect plan for your own life. We must remember that Christ is whom we serve, not an ideology or a methodology. My friend and mentor, Pastor Jerry Jones, who has since gone home with THE LORD, use to quote the great commission to me all the time when he would say that, "Christ died to establish the Church so that we may go throughout the world preaching His Gospel. Making disciples and teaching them all the things that we have learned from Him as His true followers." The simple fact remains that Christ established His Church for His purpose, and all that is required of us is our complete obedience and unquestionable commitment to Him and Him alone.

The moment we place more importance on methodology, or gatherings and our own practices, placing them above that of Christ's Purpose and Will for our lives, that's when we begin to fall short of His Glory. The moment when we make justifications for our lack and sometimes false actions is when we walk away from God's ordained faith and become nothing more than a cult. Saul used to do this until he was transformed into Paul. Indeed he reminds us why this is so in Ephesians 1:11-14 (ESV), "we have in Christ obtained an inheritance so that we who were first to hope in Christ may know that we are His children a promised that is sealed and assured by His Holy Spirit." Paul understood that this new body of believers were meant to truly be the Church of God, His people, and as a result, we must never back down from the calling of God's Church on earth, which is to spread His Gospel of hope. We must never back down from the injustices of this world and face its bullies head-on, in the power of the name of our LORD! But what can one person do, Moy?

In another one of his letters in God's inspired Word, the book of 1 Corinthians 12:12-27 (ESV), Paul expands on the idea of the Church: "For as the body is one and has many members, but all the members of that one body, being many, are one body, so also is Christ. For by one Spirit, we were all baptized into one body and have all been made to drink into one Spirit. For, in fact, the body is not one member but many... and now God has set the members, each one of them, in the body just as He pleased. But God composed the body, having given greater honor to that part which lacks it, that there should be no schism in the body, but that the members should have the same care for one another. And if one member suffers, all the members suffer with it; or if one member is honored, all the members rejoice with it. Now you are the body of Christ and members individually." Join the Church and take your part in the body of Christ!

In the lifelong wilderness of Paul, we learn that even in difficult times, we must share a message of hope based on the Scriptures. Our ministry must be motivated by the love of God that we may live a practical Christianity. Our mission must continue to be to preach the Gospel of Jesus Christ and to serve the needy in His name. The Bible truly is God's inspired Word and the clear revelation of Christ and the work of salvation that He performs on our behalf. The love which motivates us to serve comes from God's love, mercy, and grace represented by the blood on the Cross. (217Faith.Church). Therefore, our love in action, our faithful response to this mission should be to share that love, to share that hope through the courageous preaching of God's Word while at the same time extending a hand to help those who are not only suffering physically but firstly, suffering spiritually. Since our God-established beginnings, the Church was meant to be agents of God's love and mercy to a lost world as a part of His Church and not independent of it. All thought eh individual suffering and development of its miners.

The Scriptures tell us in Luke 16:13 (CEB) that "no servant can serve two masters; for either he will hate the one and love the other, or else he will be loyal to the one and have content for the other." In the end, no matter how much we may try to justify our actions, this is what it boils down to. In our lack of faith, we have failed to trust God to provide the resources we need to accomplish His mission parameter. In the established Church and our private lives, many have come to compromised their royal priesthood for the sake of money at times to please others and not God. When we do this, we walk away from our mandate and God's purpose for our lives, putting personal pride above God's Will. This is a clear case of serving two masters, and we cannot be so arrogant about this fact. This is one big reason why some people out there feel angry and want nothing to do with the established Church. Too many of its parts (denominations) of the body of Christ have become money-focused, or even service-focused or worse, self-focused instead of God-focused. When we become these things, we dismiss our God-given road map for faithful living, and we neglect the care of others, or vice versa, so much so that we get lost in our agendas and slowly slip away from God's perfect will.

As a result, our faith can become a sort of junkyard religion. Bits and pieces of old unpolished teachings that we put together to resemble a working model, but in the end, it is not a deep harmonious, meaningful, or life-transforming teaching. Be a good person, they say, just tolerate the wrong behavior of others, be dismissive of your own sins of omission. Because of this type of thinking, many walk away because of the watered-down presentation of our hope in Christ. Our congregations are dying as we celebrate our mediocrity. In Proverbs 1:32 (NASB), we read that the complaisance of the fool will destroy them. Dear reader, certainly we often gripe about our own wilderness experience, yet more often than not, we have no one else to blame but ourselves, due in great part to our faithless acts and inability to hold on to the promises of God. Even when God permits these times of trials, not many of us succeed. Yet thank God that despite us, He is good and He is faithful, and if we truly repent, He promises to restore us and utilize us for His mission of hope once again.

We must denounce the hypocrisy in our churches and our lives that as a virus has been allowed to fester and grow in the hearts and minds of many believers. As a result, many believe faith is non-existent or, as I've heard it said before, an inch deep and a mile wide instead of being the other way. No real substance or conviction is left to stand up against injustice and sin. We sacrifice context and substance for mere statistics and promotions, and we become nothing less than Pharisees in our approach to God's calling in our lives and His purpose for His Church. No wonder God allows wilderness experiences in our lives to transform us and reshape us back to His Will. Friends in our world, there is a genuine lack of love for one another. You cannot tell apart most congregants from the secular world as a consequence of the sins of pride, of gossip, the sin of backstabbing, and the sin of backsliding that we have not allowed God to deal with in us.

We must never compromise our calling and place in God's Church. This is the time to begin to trust and to believe once again in a God that promises to supply all of our needs according to His riches in Glory (Philippians 4:19 CEB). This is the time to recognize our God-ordained purpose of reaching the lost of the world and serving those in need. This is the time in our lives when we need to stand up and, with a Godly pride, proclaim that we are indeed a part of the body of Christ, a royal priesthood, called to accomplish God's purpose and never our own. Sure, God did call us, sure He knew our imperfections, our shortcomings, and still He calls us to partner with Him, to trust in Him at all times, and as such, He will transform us to accomplish such a calling!

In Ephesians 1:3 (ESV), we are told: "God our father who has blessed us with every spiritual blessing in the heavenly places in Christ." Then in 2 Corinthians 5:17 (ESV), Paul continues, "If anyone is in Christ, he is a new creation; old things have passed away; behold, all things have become new." As a part of the body of Christ, we are meant to live out our new forgiven life, "we have redemption through His blood, according to the riches of His grace." As part of the body of Christ, as members of His Church, we receive our salvation. (2 Timothy 2:10 CEB) This was one of the main tenants of Paul's preaching. Unity for the body for the sake of the Kingdom of God. We are called to be a church that moves, a people of action! Once again, In Ephesians 2:13-19 (NKJV), we are reminded that "now in Christ, we who once were far off have been brought near by the blood of Christ. For He is our peace...

So that He might reconcile us to God as one body. For through Jesus we both have access by one Spirit to the Father."

Many believers along the way, including myself, have gotten so engaged in denomination jargon, in selfish desires, that it has become a sort of wilderness experience as we have attempted to reconcile what God requires with what mere man through established institutions of faith demands of us. Hear me, please, there is nothing inherently wrong with organizational structure, but when that structure takes the place of God, we have started down a path that we won't too easily return from. Indeed, we need to give God the Glory for great things He has done. Not only has He given us His Son, but He has made us a part of His Church, His family. Oh, what a joy that with full freedom we may sing and understand the words of the old hymn, "I'm so glad am a part of the family of God, I've been washed in the fountain, cleansed by His blood. Made heirs with Jesus as we travel this sod, for I am a part of the family, the family of God."

The Apostle Paul was the type of leader who understood that when you take time to build others up, your perspective on your wilderness journey changes, from selfish thoughts of pain to hopeful thoughts of perseverance. As human beings, God calls us to multiply His image in us, understand the gifts of others, develop them, and encourage the best in others in their service to God. To grow in the Spirit to such an extent that His fruits are evident in all they do. To help others build confidence and achieve their spiritual potential. To learn from our wilderness journey and conclude that no matter how bad it may get, God's will is percent, and He will bring joy and purpose from our suffering for His honor and glory.

We must recognize our places as part of Christ's Church that we may truly be able to love our God with all of our hearts and soul and to also love our neighbors as ourselves. (Mark 12:30-31 CEB). We must never compromise our faith and service as members of this body. After all, it is what we are called to be. A church, a fellowship, a gathering of believers together, bringing honor and Glory to God in everything we do, especially in our service of others. Called to seek first His kingdom and, by definition, the things of God and to trust that He will simply add the rest. He will bless us with what we need. He will provide and supply all other necessities, no matter how terrible our wilderness journey may be. God is always faithful and good! This is something Paul understood and practiced.

Let us then begin to trust in God again to do what He says He will do and see how amazed we will be! Join me today in affirming our faith in God and not merely in our abilities. Ephesians 4:4-6 (NKJV) reminds us that "there is one body and one Spirit, just as you were called in one hope of your calling; one LORD, one faith, one baptism; one God and Father of all, who is above all, and through all, and in you all." Therefore, since there is only one God, one Spirit, and one Body in Christ, then there is only one Church, and that is the Church that Christ died to establish. Paul's wilderness experience helped indeed to solidify this Church. His lifestyle of struggle helped set a firm foundation for it, which we still enjoy today. I call upon all believers to repent and to return to God, to lay aside all and any pride, and to once again come to understand what it means to be a part of the Family of God and an integral part of His Christian Church. To work to accomplish God's purpose - salvation for the entire world - and to once again trust in Him and in His provision alone to provide for our every needs that we may go and meet the needs of others as well. I've said it before, and I'll say it again when we focus on helping others, we get our eyes off our troubles, and the blessings of God follow quickly.

If there is sin in your life, then confess it, accept God's salvation and move on in faith. I have had to do this recently in my own life. The good news is that God is still in the forgiving business. But also in the empowering and the equipping for His purpose business. Stand up and proclaim with me our membership in God's Church as His children. Stand up with me and proclaim our royal calling to accomplish God's will on this earth as members of Christ's Church. Lastly, 1 Corinthians 12:6-7 (NLT) reminds us that: "there are different ways God works in our lives, but it is the same God who does the work through us. A spiritual gift is given to each of us so that we can help each other." Your wilderness journey is sure meant to develop a deeper relationship with God and be used to bless others, minister to others, and encourage others. You may even be called to live a life-long wilderness journey for His Glory. As a result, let us humbly concede the work of God in our lives, no matter how painful and difficult it may be. He will work it out in the end; there will be no lasting harm, but only hope! (Jeremiah 29:1-13 CEB)

Let us join the Psalmist in his power prayer of conviction and surrender: "THE LORD is my solid rock, my fortress, my rescuer. My God is my rock—I take refuge in Him!—He's my shield, my salvation's strength, my place of safety. Because He is praiseworthy, I cried out to THE LORD, and I was saved from my enemies. In my distress, I cried out to THE LORD; I called to my God for help. God heard my voice from His temple; I called to Him for help, and my call reached His ears." Psalms 18:2-3, 6 CEB. The Apostle James told us to "think of the various tests we encounter as occasions for joy. After all, we know that the testing of our faith produces endurance. Let this endurance complete its work so that you may be fully mature, complete, and lacking in nothing. But anyone who needs wisdom should ask God, whose very nature is to give to everyone without a second thought, without keeping score. Wisdom will certainly be given to those who ask. Whoever asks shouldn't hesitate. They should ask in faith, without doubting." James 1:2-6 (CEB)

Do not waste your Wilderness experience, my fellow traveler, but allow God to use it for His honor and Glory and so that others may be encouraged. Paul did! Even in prison, he still proclaimed:

"Brothers and sisters, I want you to know that the things that have happened to me have actually advanced the Gospel. Most of the brothers and sisters have had more confidence through THE LORD to speak the Word boldly and bravely because of my jail time." (Philippians 1:12-14 CEB). May we discover the strength of God in our weakness to get through our wilderness journey and emerge a more useful and faithful servant of God,

Dear God, please grant us the SERENITY to concede to the things we cannot change with the strength to accept them. But even the things that we must not dare to change, such as Your Calling and Purpose for each of us. Please grant us the COURAGE to change the things we can change (like ourselves) with the resolve to do so. Courage to learn from our journeys and tell others of Your good news of salvation for a lost world by serving their needs. And please, Father, grant us the WISDOM to boldly know the difference. To always seek You in prayer and worship as members of your Christian body of believers. It is indeed in Christ alone that we will place our trust. LORD, bring us understanding and conviction as we work through these teachings concerning your work of grace in our lives. Help us use the gifts you have granted us to develop your Church here on earth. Father, allow Your Spirit to teach us to edify You and to continue to prepare us and mold us into the faithful and obedient follower of Christ that You call us to be. For it is in Christ's name and for His Glory that we pray. Amen!

Questions to keep exploring.

Are you familiar with the serenity prayer? (Search it if you are not) How can it help to bring peace to your life during your trials?

Is there something in your past that still lingers in your mind today and brings you guilt?

Have you tried confessing to God?

How can you improve upon the Church's work as a member of the body of Christ in your community and circles of influence?

In faith, how do you believe God will use your spiritual journey to bring peace and comfort to the lives of others?

12

―――――◆•◆•◆―――――

SO, NOW WHAT?

I'm sure about this: the one who started a good
work in you will stay with you to complete the job
by the day of Christ Jesus. Philippians 1:6 (CEB)

I n my option, the movie Tomorrowland with George Clooney became an instant sci-fi sensation. The movie is based on the Disneyland park idea where Walt Disney had dreamed of gathering all the smartest and most passionate people to build a better future for all, free of the limitations and restrictions of government, greed, or misguided ideas. In the movie, a machine created in this utopia of science begins to predict the end of the world. It turns out that the machine itself was feeding negative thoughts back towards earth, and so folks were living out a self-fulfilling prophesy. They felt the world was going to end, so they found a way to make it happen.

In the movie, the character of Casey Newton, a passionate and intelligent young woman who believed something could still be done to correct the path humanity was on, recalls a story her father had told her since she was a young girl. She reminds her dad of the two wolves that are always at odds with each other. One is sadness and despair, and the other is joy and hope. She then asked, which wolf wins, dad? To which her dad responds, the one you feed will win. If you feed your despair, you will become depressed, but if you feed hope, you will live in anticipation of God's mercies and that He will do what He has promised to do according to scripture. In our wilderness experience, it's always easy to feed despair, after all, poor me right", but have you tried feeding your hope? This will prove especially difficult to do when we are at our lowest point. Try it, be hopeful, wait patiently and seek to know what God intends to do in you and through you even during your terrible situation. According to scripture, one of the three greatest things in life is Joy, Hope, and Love! (1 Corinthians 13:13 CEB) Yes, love is the greatest, but only when experienced through a hopeful and joyful heart.

One of the main lessons that I have learned in my own wilderness experience is that my trial may not be completed until I learn to live in hope. An integral part of this life of hope is learning to forgive others and ourselves. Yes, forgiveness will free our souls and minds to better focus on the source of that forgiveness, Jesus Christ. Forgiveness allows us to redirect our desires for vengeance towards a cheating or unkind spouse, a mean-spirited, negative boss, even a selfish or self-centered attitude in our own lives. It is a forgiveness that is not only necessarily directed towards others but also towards ourselves. Think about it, what guilt, what shame, what blame have you assigned yourself, preventing you from forgiving yourself? When you repent and confess your actions to God, He forgives you. After all, Jesus died for our sin, and the Holy Spirit bathes us in His prevenient grace that we may turn to and trust in God once and for all.

So what are you doing with that knowledge? Release yourself, surrender yourself into the arms of an all-loving God, and forgive yourself. Maybe you were at fault for what is happening to you;

forgive yourself anyway, Jesus has! Maybe you had nothing to do with what is taking place in your life and got caught up in the shuffles, well forgive others, and trust that God can and will deal with them in His way. God forgives us, we must do the same for others and ourselves, otherwise that forgiveness is not real in us. I sought forgiveness once from those I blamed for my struggles, and it was denied, yet that did not stop God from forgiving me for the poor choices that have followed. He forgave me and has been working in my own life to forgive them.

Wilderness experiences never last forever. God's will is always accomplished on the other side of our struggles. No matter what, learn to trust in the Lord and lean not on your own understanding. He will never leave you but goes before you. He will provide for your needs because He has a beautiful, hope-filled plan just for you. We are never alone. He prepares a way for us, He is with us, and He sends others along the way to help us through. If God went through all this trouble for these His servant that we have studied in this book, what makes you think He is not ready to do the same in you. To bring you through the desert, cleansed, refined, rehabilitated, prepared, and full of hopeful perseverance. Just like God was found by the prophet in the whisper and not the other loud occurrence! We may experience the amazing grace of God in the details of life. Let us intentionally look for and focus on the little things, for they represent the small steps on the path out of our wilderness experience into the marvelous light of God. The light where God's big picture for you and me will make sense and where we will be better equipped to serve Him in our service of others!

Understanding God's timing is everything. Knowing when to move is crucial. What we do is important, but when we do it, let's others know where we place our trust. As you travel through your wilderness, please spend time seeking clarity from God. Bathe yourself in prayer and be still as God prepares others around you for what He will accomplish through you. The timing of our response must be perfect as the LORD opens doors and creates opportunities for us. The Apostle Paul reminds his student Timothy and us what we should do next: how we should live our lives.

In his letter to the Ephesians, we read in chapter 6 verses 10-18 CEB: "Finally, be strengthened by the Lord and his powerful strength. Put on God's armor so that you can make a stand against the tricks of the devil. We aren't fighting against human enemies but against rulers, authorities, forces of cosmic darkness, and spiritual powers of evil in the heavens. Therefore, pick up the full armor of God so that you can stand your ground on an evil day and after you have done everything possible to still stand. So stand with the belt of truth around your waist, justice as your breastplate, and put shoes on your feet so that you are ready to spread the good news of peace. Above all, carry the shield of faith so that you can extinguish the flaming arrows of the evil one. Take the helmet of salvation and the sword of the Spirit, which is God's word. Offer prayers and petitions in the Spirit all the time. Stay alert by hanging in there and praying for all believers."

The Word of God once again puts it all in perspective in Hebrew 5:7-8 MSG, "While He lived on earth, anticipating death, Jesus cried out in pain and wept in sorrow as He offered up priestly prayers to God. Because He honored God, God answered him. Though He was God's Son, He learned trusting obedience by what He suffered, just as we do." If Jesus needed to experience suffering, well, it just doesn't leave any room for complaining. How will we dare to skip this class if He had to take it? Simply said, suffering will be a part of our education as God's children. This is not to say that every bad thing that comes our way is God's discipline. It does not mean that marital crisis is some sort of retribution for past sins. That is bad theology, and it has hurt a lot of people. We are all responsible for our own choices. We still live in a sinful world, where sometimes well-intentioned people suffer, and misguided people get away with murder!

A friend was suffering from a terrible flu; she said, "I sure hope I learn what God has for me in this so that I can get over it." I didn't want to be unkind, so I kept my mouth shut. But inside, I thought, you think God made you sick!? There are other things at work in this world. Germs and viruses, for instance. Organisms that could sure be a consequence of the original sin, but now, I tend to doubt. Can God use the sickness in your life for a His good? Absolutely. But is He making you sick? I highly doubt it.

We live in a broken world; disease, accident, injury are just part of life outside of Eden. This world has foul spirits in it, too; they cause a lot of havoc. The sin of man is also enough to sink any ship. Stir all these together, and you got plenty of reason for suffering. So don't go thinking that every bad thing happening is God punishing you. As Dallas Willard reminds us, "What we learn about God from Jesus should prove to us that suffering and 'bad things happening to us are not the Father's preferred way of dealing with us, sometimes necessary, perhaps, but never what He prefers."

Sometimes we wish we could have a heads up when our troubles are coming. I used to play this game from time to time called boom beach, and ever so often, when I would try to log in to play, a window would pop up, and it would say, "you are currently under attack; your base will load when it is finished." Once you could get back in, the base would always be utterly destroyed. They take your resources, your game points. But, it always reloads, it always comes back to normal, it always gives you a chance to rearrange your game plan, to fortify your defenses, to try a different strategy. In a very real way, this is what wilderness experiences are. They give us opportunities, yes, be it a painful one at times, to rethink our tactics, come up with a new approach and bring our lives back into better alignment and synchronization with God's purpose for us.

One final item to add. I'm writing these words from a broken place but also a place of healing and restoration. Do I hope this will stop completely soon, every day! Do I pray the lessons required will be learned by me sooner rather than later? Absolutely! Do I believe in my heart that ultimately God is in control and will see me through it all for His honor and glory? More and more, I would say, without a doubt!!! I can testify that while at first, I could not see past the nose in my face, through this process, God has filled me with hope, a hopeful perseverance that allows me to keep moving forward through His plans as He leads me.

Although they may be valid, we can sometimes ask the wrong question, such as when will my trials end? When instead, we should ask, how can I better serve you, LORD, what in me must still change, what rough edge must still be sanded down, what must I do to be more Christlike and even if you do not rescue me? Yet, even after all of our questions have gone answered, we must still proclaim our faithful loyalty to God and our unquestionable faith in His goodwill for our lives. This achievement will not be easy and may never be fully completed until we stand in the presence of God one day. Nonetheless, we must not stop loving Jesus, being obedient to God our Father, and relying with fully repentant hearts in the guiding of the Holy Spirit. God is rooting for us, in fact, there is a cloud of witnesses, those who have gone before us, who are cheering us along, out of our wilderness experiences, into the perfect Will of God! As a result, let us lay our sin aside and trust in God's goodness, His mercy, and grace. (Hebrew 12:2, CEB)

Seek God's mercies through prayers. Not a mere to-do list that you present and expect Him to deliver at the end of business day, no, but truly develop two-way communication with your Father in heaven who loves you very much. Some things may have happened to you that you honestly did not deserve, or maybe not to the degree that you experienced hardship because of it. Yet, God can still use that situation for good in your life. I got my family back! Thank you, Father! I got my faith in Jesus back, even though

I still struggle with the events of my past, thank you, Holy Sprint. But will I ever get my full-time ministry back? I hope so, I pray so, I wish so, I want so, I need so. Yet, maybe not, and perhaps God is opening new avenues for me to minister and share my testimony of hope through my writing that others like you may find comfort and joy. I truly hope so! More recently, God has led us to an online base ministry effort through Facebook, Zoom, Youtube and Spotify called 217Faith. Also online at www.217Faith.church. Please drop by and say hello!

As I have learned about God's goodness and faithfulness so far, as I have seen Him rebuilding and fortifying my character and maturing my faith, I must admit that even if these other things I still hope for do not come to be, I must still be ever so willing to serve God in whatever other way possible and never let the attack's of the enemy or the negativity of others push me away from my good Heavenly Father. He will provide for my every need you see; this I know for sure. He will never leave me or forsake me, even if I get so lost in my own struggles; this I also know to be true. His will for me is good, full of hope, and what else do I need but hope.

Thank you, Father, for this journey I have traveled so far. Even if more refining is needed, more correction may still be necessary, more chiseling of my impurities, more of the dross of my pass may still need to be painfully removed, then so be it. When I am week, you are strong, and with you, I can do all things. (Philippians 4:13 CEB). Please grant me strength to be exactly who you purposed me to be, that I may give you the honor and glory only you deserve. Make it so, Father, I pray.

We've looked at eleven Bible characters and their wilderness experience journey. From them, we've learned;

1) God still has a purpose for us, even when we mess up.

2) Even when we don't deserve it, our pain can ultimately reveal the greatness of God.
3) Our suffering may be there just so that others can experience the compassion of God.
4) A shared experience can encourage us to carry on and never stop carrying for what really matters.
5) Our journey through the unknown is always part of God's greater plan for His people.
6) Even after sin, we can come to please God and continue in His journey for our lives.
7) Rebuilding is a team sport, just follow God's blueprint and don't be afraid to ask others for help and support.
8) Obedience always leads to salvation and restoration, despite our situations.
9) Restoration is always God's purpose for His children.
10) Complete transformations and character development are God's specialty.
11) Faithful perseverance will always lead us to God's grace and fill us with His hope.

There are still many other biblical characters and their wilderness experiences that we could have included, and so I offer them to you as honorable mentions to encourage you to continue your study on this subject and fortify further your faith in our merciful God who truly longs to be merciful to you. (Isaiah 30:18 CEB)

Noah. A wilderness experience brought upon by obedience. He literally floated away as the world was being destroyed. Yet God remembered him and fulfilled His promises to humanity through the faithfulness of one man and his family. (Genesis 8 CEB) Truly a new beginning.

Jacob. A wilderness experience brought upon by deception. From birth, this man wiggles his way to a place of honor, a place of birthright! He even had a little wrestling match with God himself!

Yet through it all, God was with him and granted him a great vision for His family's future. Establishing through his suffering what would become the twelve tribes of the Nation of Israel. (Genesis 28:15-16 CEB)

Joshua. A wilderness experience was brought upon by following a great man of God. Even though his faith never waivers, he still wonders the land for forty years. All along, being trained to take over and lead God's people into the promised land. (Joshua 1:1-9 CEB)

Gideon. A wilderness journey experienced in doubt and worry, in thoughts of inability and insecurity. Gideon thought himself so unworthy of God, and yet, in the end, God used him and a handful of brave men to defeat an entire army and establish the power of God over his enemies. Ultimately, his journey reminds him that surrendering to God in full confidence is the best and only option for the servant of God. (Judges 6-8)

Samson. A wilderness experience that led him from one selfish behavior to another. From pride to anger, from disobedience to entitlement, and from arrogance to humiliation. Samson, however, shows us the extent of God's goodness and hope and how He can always use a willing heart to fulfill His purpose, even if it results in the death of the servant. It makes me wonder what sort of celebration they had in heaven after Samson finally got it right and made it home! (Judges 13-16)

Jonah. He resisted God's purpose for his life to such a degree that he tried to run away from God! His perception of how God's mercy worked did now allow him to see the generosity of God. However, he came through and eventually became obedient, yet we sadly leave Jonah deep in his own wilderness, still desiring his perceptions to become a reality rather than God's will. I pray that God ultimately showed great mercy to Jonah's stubbornness and resistance and that perhaps he found peace in God's grace towards others.

Daniel and His crew! They all had their own wilderness journeys. Daniel got to hang out with hungry lions (Daniel 6), while his friends Shadrach, Meshach, and Abednego stood in the middle of a fiery furnace with God. Yet, they all survived and were able to testify of the faithfulness and mercy of God. (Daniel 3:16-28 CEB). They all understood the simple fact that God could save them, and yet even if God chose not to do so, they would remain faithful to God, no questions asked!

Jeremiah preached a message of hope even as he found himself in exile that still speaks to our weary Hearst's today. God's promises are evident through Jeremiah. At the potter's house, God shows him how he can mold, create, break and reshape us all if we allow him (Jeremiah 18:1-11 CEB). Later on, God's promise that the people's exile would not be there forever and His reminder that He always has a plan for His children and that if we seek Him, we will indeed find him! (Jeremiah 29:10-13 CEB)

Esther. In exile herself, forced into an arranged marriage, she eventually would be responsible for saving the people of God. Her hope, encouraged by her uncle, allowed her to do what was right, speak up against bullies, and hope that God was not done with His people. She moved in faith, and God acted! She may have also been responsible for the return of God's people back to the Promised Land.

Mary and Joseph. Be careful that when God makes you a promise, you make no assumptions about how easy life will get from then on! From a life-changing revelation about giving birth to the Son of God. Being chased away because someone wanted to kill their boy, wandering through foreign lands playing the waiting game. To finally experiencing the death of their child and ultimately coming to understand the why of it all and fully trusting in God's plan through their unbelievable journey of faith!

Well, this is quite the journey we have been on! I know that God is not done with me, and perhaps He may not be fully done until the day I stand before Him in glory, and you know what, that's ok! Because no matter what dark valley I may be asked to walk through, no matter what unforeseen pain or sorrow may still be in my future, no matter what God may allow others to do to me, or how empty and completely lost I may feel, I know without a doubt that He is with me and will never leave me, I know that His mercies are new every morning. I know that He will comfort me and stand by me so that together God may transform me into the servant He has always wanted me to be. I pray that you can come to believe, despite your circumstances, that God desires the same things for you, and most importantly, if you surrender to His will, right now, He will begin His work of grace this very moment.

Trust me, from experience, I can say there is no better place to be than in the loving arms of Jesus, especially when we are called to travel in the wilderness, if just for a time! Keep an open heart and mind in your journey. Be obedient as He leads you. When I stepped down from my ministry and moved to beautiful Florida, I struggled to find work until I eventually landed at Walmart as a part-time cashier. Honestly, I did not want to be there; my pride told me I deserved so much more. Still, I took the position. It seems to me now that God was in the details all along. Within two and half years, I had been promoted up to Assistant Manager, and as I write these words, I've been promoted yet again. Then, I suddenly became an essential person in the middle of the Covid pandemic. During times where so many had suffered loss of jobs and income, God has provided for all of my needs, and it started with a simple step of obedience to take a job that I didn't really want to do. A step forward in hope out of a very dark spiritual place. Remember, God always plays the long game, make sure to move in obedience, and He will not disappoint you.

God bless you as you seek to grow in your walk of faith, hope, and Holiness (Christlikeness)! Much like the accounts of this book, faith and hope have been proven to be achievable Christian characters for the child of God who seeks Him regardless of their difficulties. The last attribute of Holiness is also achievable by faithful action and right living. There is a great line in the movie "The Kingdom of Heaven" where the protagonist proclaims that he had lost his religion, to which the priest responds that he cares not for religion but instead speaks of living a life of Holiness. Then he says: "Holiness is in right action, and courage on behalf of those who cannot defend themselves, and goodness. God desires a right mind and a contrite hears (italic is mine). What you decide to do every day, you will be a good person - or not." May the studies in this book set you loose to go forward in the full assurance of God's work in us to live right that He may indeed use you for the benefit of His Kingdom, even amid trials. Be guided by the encouragement of the great Apostles Paul himself in his letter to the Romans chapter 5 verses 1-11 (CEB):

"Therefore, since we have been made righteous through his faithfulness, we have peace with God through our Lord Jesus Christ. We have access by faith into this grace in which we stand through him, and we boast in the hope of God's glory.

But not only that! We even take pride in our problems because trouble produces endurance, endurance produces character, and character produces hope.

This hope doesn't put us to shame because the love of God has been poured out in our hearts through the Holy Spirit, who has been given to us. While we were still weak, at the right moment, Christ died for ungodly people.

It isn't often that someone will die for a righteous person, though maybe someone might dare die for a good person. But God shows his love for us because while we were still sinners, Christ died for us. So, now that we have been made righteous by his blood, we can be even more certain that we will be saved from God's wrath through him.

If we were reconciled to God through the death of his Son while we were still enemies, now that we have been reconciled, how much more certain is it that we will be saved by his life? And not only that: we even take pride in God through our Lord Jesus Christ, the one through whom we now have a restored relationship with God."

Keep hoping friends; it is the greatest tool available to us all, no matter what stage of our journey we may be at. Hope will see you through faith will hold you strong, and Holiness will be how others will know you have remained faithful to God.

"The LORD bless you and protect you.
The LORD make His face shine on you
and be gracious to you.
The LORD lift up His face to you
and grant you peace."

Numbers 6:24-26 (CEB)

ABOUT THE AUTHOR

Born to Christian parents and grandparents, Moy grew up in a loving Christian home throughout all of his life. As a young man, he taught Sunday school classes, sang in the choirs, and worked side by side with his parents at opening churches. Eventually, the time came when he followed in his ancestral steps and attended seminary school with The Salvation Army, where he was ordained and commissioned as an officer and for fourteen years had several Senior Pastor appointments in the Southern California area. There he met his beautiful wife Erika and soon had two children Jocy and Josh. Moy attended Azusa Pacific University, where he received a Bachelor of Science degree in Organizational Leadership, and later on a Masters of Arts degree in Human Resources and Organizational Development. Eventually, life brought him and his family down to Central Florida, where he was ordained once again now by the Free Methodist Church, USA. These days Moy works as an Academy Coach for Walmart, where he has the opportunity to train new Managers. Moy has written one other book titled "Praying Through the Psalms." His heart's desire remains to serve God by sharing His Word and the service of those in need. Together with his wife, they lead an online-based ministry encouraging believers to put their faith in action.

You may join the efforts online at:
www.217Faith.Church

Printed in the United States
by Baker & Taylor Publisher Services